Michigan
CURIOSITIES

Help Us Keep This Guide Up to Date

Every effort has been made by the authors and editors to make this guide as accurate and useful as possible. However, many things can change after a guide is published—establishments close, phone numbers change, hiking trails are rerouted, facilities come under new management, and so on.

We would appreciate hearing from you concerning your experiences with this guide and how you feel it could be improved and kept up to date. While we may not be able to respond to all comments and suggestions, we'll take them to heart, and we'll also make certain to share them with the authors. Please send your comments and suggestions to the following address:

GPP
Reader Response/Editorial Department
PO Box 480
Guilford, CT 06437
Or you may e-mail us at:
editorial@globepequot.com
Thanks for your input, and happy travels!

Curiosities Series

Michigan
CURIOSITIES

Quirky characters,
roadside oddities &
other offbeat stuff

Third Edition

Colleen Burcar

Guilford, Connecticut

To the engaging, big-hearted people featured in this book who graciously allowed me to label them as Michigan Curiosities.

To my parents, Mary and John Burcar, who, having taught me the pleasures of traveling both peninsulas of our Great Lakes State, are now on a heavenly journey of their own as my newest guardian angels.

The prices and rates in this guidebook were confirmed at press time. We recommend, however, that you call establishments before traveling to obtain current information.

To buy books in quantity for corporate use or incentives, call **(800) 962–0973** or e-mail **premiums@GlobePequot.com**.

Text design: Bret Kerr
Layout artist: Casey Shain
Project editor: Lauren Brancato
Maps by Melissa Baker © Morris Book Publishing, LLC
All photos by Colleen Burcar unless otherwise noted.

ISSN 1542-2283

ISBN 978-0-7627-6978-0

Printed in the United States of America

10 9 8 7 6 5 4 3 2

about the author

Colleen Burcar has worked as a reporter in radio, television, and newspapers for many years. Thirteen of those years were spent working alongside Gene Taylor, sharing comic banter. She now works in media consulting and public relations while her voice continues to be heard on commercials across the country. She's the author of *You Know You're in Michigan When . . .* and shares her love of Michigan in public speaking engagements across the state. The mother of a daughter, Kimberly, Colleen currently resides in suburban Detroit with her husband, Bryan Becker, and toy poodle, Chloe.

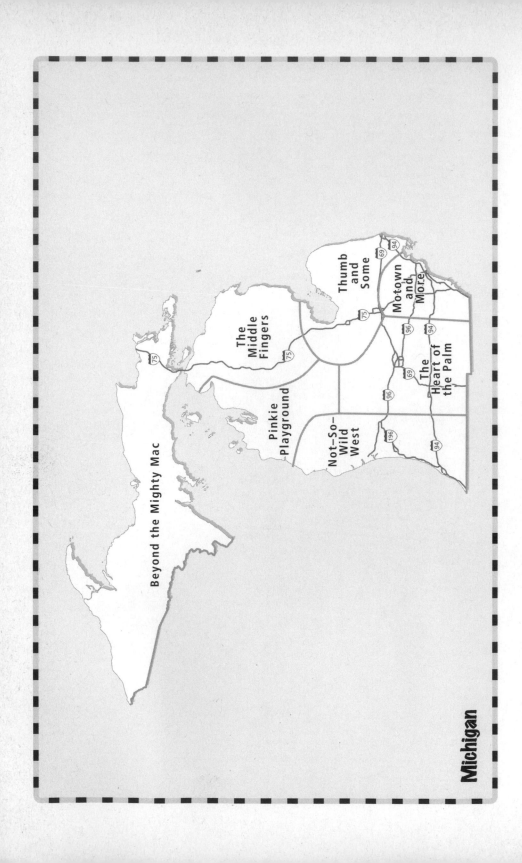

Michigan

Beyond the Mighty Mac

The Middle Fingers

Thumb and Some

Motown and More

Pinkie Playground

Not-So-Wild West

The Heart of the Palm

contents

acknowledgments

⭐ ⭐

I'd first like to thank Cindy Snyder and Mary Sue Brooks (now retired after thirty-five years) of Travel Michigan for getting me started in the right direction on my quest for *Michigan Curiosities*. Thank you to Dianna Stampfler, formerly of the West Michigan Tourist Association, a dynamic lady who constantly fed me with food for creative thought. My gratitude also goes out to Shirley Roberts of Bay City; Barb Williams of the Four Flags Area; Carol Potter of Cadillac; Cynthia Asiala of Project Kaleva; Len Trankina of Mackinac Island; Bob Tagatz, historian and concierge at The Grand Hotel; Traverse City radio personality Ron Jolly; Barry Godwin; Peter Fitzsimons of Petoskey Harbor Springs, Boyne Country; Renee Harlow of Marshall; Dean Woodbeck of Houghton; and the scores of others who helped by providing me with priceless tips about the undiscovered treasures in our state.

Thanks to all my family and friends who didn't see me for months yet continued to provide me with wacky ideas to research, especially techno wizard Steve Kranson, Carol and Tom Beeler, Lin Cargo, Donna Joseph, Mary and Diana Nowak, Annette and Dave Mullet, and Marilyn and David Lochner. A special thanks to Lin Celko for giving me the opportunity to write this book and Gene Taylor's wife, Helen Pasakarnis, who gave the project the green light and encouraged me every step of the way. A resounding "merci beaucoup" to Andy Dubill, my friend since kindergarten, with whom I share similar ancestral roots firmly planted in the Upper Peninsula. His inquisitive nature and insatiable appetite for the pursuit of quirky Michigan adventures proved to be both invaluable and profoundly appreciated.

A heartfelt thanks to my traveling companion, best friend, and husband, Bryan Becker, who drove thousands of miles around Michigan, offering support, insight, understanding, and love. And finally, thanks to Chloe, our four-pound toy poodle, who, for the sake of quiet curiosity, allowed herself to be smuggled into countless Michigan hotels.

preface

*A*llow me to introduce you to Michigan, also known as the Wolverine State, although there hasn't been any sight of the stocky weasel here in years, and perhaps never was. Rumor has it that during the Toledo War of 1835 (settled without a fight—Ohio got Toledo, we got the Upper Peninsula) an Ohioan got mad and referred to Michigan residents as wolverines, distant cousins of the skunk. The term stuck and went on to become the name of both the official mascot of the University of Michigan and, ironically for many years, the yearbook at rival Michigan State University.

Whatever you want to call me as a 100 percent Michigan homegrown product, I'm proud to be a resident of the nation's twenty-sixth state, the only state in the nation split into two parts. My loyalty to the 96,705 square miles within Michigan's hand-shaped boundaries has never wavered. Born and bred here, I've never had the desire to live anywhere else.

The things that identify me as an authentic local are the same things that make it easy to pick out anybody else from Michigan: I play both pinochle and euchre (although I have a terrible time remembering how to spell either) and can claim at least one friend who's been a queen of some local fruit or vegetable festival. Credit for the latter goes to my buddy Tamara Van Wormer Tazzia who, as Miss Pinconning's Cheese Queen of some years back, went on to become Munger's Potato Queen. To this day, she still savors potatoes, the cheesier the better.

Now that I've verified myself as an honest-to-goodness Michiganian, validating my participation in the writing of a book on oddities in the state, I must tell you that this assignment wasn't, and really isn't, mine. The project originally belonged to Gene Taylor, an incredibly talented man with whom I had the privilege to work for thirteen years.

Frankly, there was no one better than Gene to take on this task, as he himself could be characterized as the quintessential Michigan curiosity. Dressed in his trademark bow tie and ready to work at 5:00 a.m., Gene would spend afternoons cantering through meadows on horseback, followed by evenings serving as master of ceremonies at local charity events. On Wednesdays time after work was filled with service to the

Conducting his own "Elvis for President" campaign,
Gene Taylor, in a snowy white jumpsuit, was the
consummate "good humor man."
HELEN PASAKARNIS

Salvation Army, where he'd dish up food to the needy as a regular on the Bed and Bread Truck.

Every wedding needs an Elvis impersonator and, thanks to Gene, mine had the best. His rockin' version of "Blue Suede Shoes" will forever live in my memory as (almost) the most memorable part of the night. No one could keep up with him on the dance floor, as much as we tried. Gene and I once entered a dance contest and, disappointingly, placed second. I'm sure it was my fault we didn't win, since Gene had hip-swinging gyrations that even the King couldn't emulate.

After more than a decade in radio together and several years in television working on *Good Afternoon Detroit* (where he was known as "The Wise Guy"), I was personally grateful for Gene's persistence in bolstering my confidence in my own journalistic skills. If it wasn't for him, I might never have taken a writing position with the *Detroit News*.

Through the years our paths crossed many times—personally, professionally, and even spiritually as members of the Detroit chapter of Christian Media Fellowship. But I was not remotely prepared for the directions our lives would take us next.

In January 2001, with notebook in hand, enthusiastically writing this, his first book, Gene Taylor's life on earth came to an end. News of his untimely passing brought shock and sorrow to the entire Detroit area. His pen and the project had been silenced.

What began as a mournful year continued. Within six months, I faced several unexpected personal losses. Then one night, out of the blue, I was approached by Linda Celko of Globe Pequot Press. She asked if I'd be interested in completing the *Michigan Curiosities* project. It was obviously divine intervention at work. The book that had been abruptly closed would now be reopened.

Perhaps the manner in which this project fell into my lap could be considered a Michigan curiosity in itself. And so with the blessing of Gene's wife, Helen Pasakarnis, I picked up the pen and finished writing a book that I believe Gene, with his zest for life and unique sense of humor, would have appreciated. I hope you enjoy the results.

—Colleen Burcar

introduction

★ ★

By Gene Taylor

Michigan is a curiosity, or at least full of them. Maybe *contradictions* is a better word, but who'd buy a book titled *Michigan Contradictions*? This is a state where we named a car after a president (Lincoln) and a president after a car (Ford). It's the Wolverine State but has no wolverines. Not only can you drive south from Michigan to Canada, if you've got the time, you can drive to Hell (Michigan) and back.

We're the only people in the country who use our hands as a map to point out where we live. On the plus side, we never lose a map and it's a nice change of pace to have people use their entire hand to tell you where to go. And while we call Michigan the Winter Wonderland, we've got more public golf courses than any state in the Union, as well as more registered boats than Florida or California.

Michigan is home to the world's largest, most unusual car show. There are incredible dream cars everywhere, but no one will try to sell you a car.

Detroit's Woodward Dream Cruise every August draws tens of thousands of custom cars and more than a million people to stand on Woodward Avenue and watch them drive by. You can see cars with engines so powerful they can pass anything except a gas station. On that summer weekend the clock is turned back to the days of poodle skirts, fuzzy dice hanging from rearview mirrors, and more oil in guys' hair than under their hoods.

Michigan could have been the inspiration for Bambi's mother saying, "Man is in the forest." Every November, hundreds of thousands of deer hunters spend lots of dough and big bucks to try to shoot a doe or get a big buck.

Where else but our mitten-shaped peninsula would you have a city named Novi that has that name to this day because somebody misread a stagecoach map that said the stop was No. VI? (That's number "6" in Roman numerals.)

introduction

Canada is north of the United States, but when you drive to Canada from Detroit, you head south to Windsor, Ontario. And as any Detroiter will explain to you, Windsor is really just a suburb of Detroit with different money and stronger beer.

Michiganians eat Coney Island hot dogs that are nothing like hot dogs served on Coney Island, and consume hundreds of thousands of massive Polish jelly doughnuts in a single insane celebration called Paczki Day; waiters in Greek restaurants celebrate their heritage by lighting cheese, a tradition practically unknown in Greece.

In an election year, pundits will tell you that Michigan is a battleground state. That's because this state is a microcosm of America. When politicians talk about "solid midwestern values," they mean the people here, who work hard and play harder.

Michigan is a collection of the wild and wonderful people, the places they go, and the things they say and do. Over the next few pages, I'd like to introduce you to *Michigan Curiosities*.

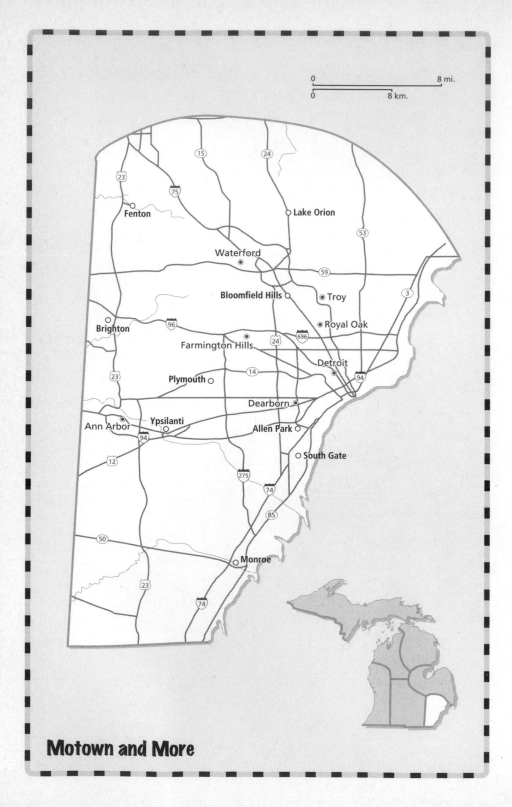

0   8 mi.
0   8 km.

23

15   24

75

Fenton   Lake Orion

53

Waterford

59

Bloomfield Hills   Troy

3

96

Royal Oak

Brighton

24   696

Farmington Hills

Detroit

23   14

Plymouth   94

Dearborn

Ann Arbor   Ypsilanti   Allen Park

94

South Gate

12

275

74

85

50

Monroe

23

74

Motown and More

1

Motown and More

Although Antoine Laumet *de la Monthe Cadillac is given credit for founding Detroit in 1701, he was probably just the first to get enough cash from French king Louis XIV to build a fort using the brilliant rationale, "Hey, if we don't do it, the Brits will." So Louis forked over the twelve grand and Cadillac was off to Motown.*

Detroit is French for "strait," and this crooked strait connected Lake St. Clair and Lake Erie. Antoine would probably be a bit surprised by what most people consider Detroit these days.

According to the New York Times, it's the area that swings Michigan and chooses presidents. Sports Illustrated has called it the NFL coaching counterpart to the elephant burial ground. Truck drivers first called it Motown as an abbreviation for "Motortown," and former auto assembly-line worker Berry Gordy turned it into a fortune. Rolling Stone magazine says Detroit audiences are the greatest rock 'n' roll audiences in the world.

But to me, it's a curiosity gold mine.

And it's a pretty sizable gold mine, composed of eight counties and five million people living in more than 250 separate and distinct municipalities. That's a lot of politicians.

No matter where you look in Detroit, there is something automotive in your face. Visitors coming in from Metro Airport know they're in a "car town" when they're greeted by an eighty-foot giant tire that was, in its former life, a Ferris wheel at the 1964 New York World's Fair. The twelve-ton tire has been flat-free sitting along Interstate 94 since 1966.

The thing that makes Detroiters interested in an eighty-foot tire is they can just imagine the size of the car it would have to sit under. Detroiter Tim Allen (now the voice of the Pure Michigan campaign) wasn't the first to grunt, "More size, more horsepower!"

That whole "Detroit horsepower" attitude isn't an act with Tim. He's the first one to tell you he's a car guy (the Detroit counterpart to being a good ol' boy down south). To this day Tim loves cars and everything about them. The last time I saw Tim a few years ago, it was at Waterford Hills Race Track just north of Detroit. It was a weekend of historic races. And what was the multimillionaire Hollywood star driving among the classic race cars?

A tricked-out Chevy "Hello-Ralph-Nader" Corvair. That, my friends, is a big time Dee-troit car guy.

Freeway Royalty Always Tired
Allen Park

There's one tire out there that surpasses any extended warranty, having seen well beyond 50,000 miles and personally transporting two million people around its treads. It's the giant Uniroyal Tire loftily watching over motorists along the Interstate 94 corridor in Allen Park. At eight stories tall and twelve tons, it's grandiose enough to fit any SUV that automakers may be considering in the future.

Detroit's best-known billboard, wheeling with longevity.

★ ★

A shocker for some, the tire came into this world as a Ferris wheel, for the U.S. Rubber pavilion at the 1964 World's Fair in New York. Twenty-four barrel-shaped gondolas carried ninety-six people on each trip circling its circumference, including many of the well heeled. It's been said the Shah of Iran and Jacqueline Kennedy with her two young children, Caroline and John Jr., were among those burning rubber toward the sky.

OHOWIH8OHIOST8

The rivalry between alumni of Michigan State University and the University of Michigan has never been a laughing matter for die-hard fans. Either you bleed green or you're true blue through and through, and you'll do almost anything to prove your devotion.

In the 1970s, as chairman of the Michigan State Highway Department, U of M grad Peter Fletcher was taking a lot of heat for granting permission to have the Mackinac Bridge repainted green and white. What? His colleagues were appalled to learn that the team colors of the chairman's archrival would now be boldly displayed on the world's longest suspension bridge. How could such a thing be allowed to happen?

Turning a few shades of red, Fletcher decided to surreptitiously put his own stamp of loyalty into his work. While working on a new state highway map to commemorate the opening of Detroit's Renaissance Center, he persuaded a somewhat nervous cartographer, who shall remain nameless, to give birth to a few new cities that only Wolverine fans could appreciate. When the 1978 official state map

When the fair closed, the tire emerged as Humpty Dumpty, broken into 188 separate parts for transport to Detroit and requiring four months to be put back together again.

Permanent placement was found as a freeway billboard outside Uniroyal's sales office. A little cosmetic surgery (an updated hubcap) was performed, followed by work from a color stylist (neon highlights), and

was introduced, within the Ohio border were two clandestine towns named Goblu and Beatosu. So what? Nothing was done to falsify the Michigan map. Everything within state lines remained totally accurate.

More than a million copies were distributed, although most today appear to be missing in action. One of the few remaining recently was auctioned off for $1,200.

If by chance you spot an official Michigan highway map lying around from 1978 with a picture of the towers of the Renaissance Center on the cover, look closely near Bono, Ohio, just east of Toledo. Find the fictitious Goblu on it and you've got one of the originals, likely worth a lot of money.

A cautionary note: You can't judge a map by its cover. Be sure to carefully check out the insides. There are before-Fletcher and after-Fletcher versions, the latter sans the bogus Buckeye listings.

Decades later Fletcher, now president of the Credit Bureau of Ypsilanti, still gets teased about the episode, which only strengthens the pride in his Wolverine smile.

then four years later it got nailed—literally. In 1998, as a promotional gimmick for the company's new NailGard tire, a ten-foot-long, five-hundred-pound nail was hammered into its side. But a million dollar makeover plucked the nail out. In 2003 the nail sold on eBay for $3,000—the proceeds went to the Allen Park Historical Society.

Uniroyal left town some time ago. The plant was demolished in 1985, but the wheeling wonder remains as a symbol of strength for today's automotive industry.

Designed to withstand hurricane winds, the tire can be seen standing through rain, snow, sleet, or hail, on eastbound Interstate 94, east of Southfield, just a few miles from Detroit Metro Airport.

And the Winner of the World's Ugliest Trophy Is . . .
Ann Arbor—East Lansing

Without a doubt, the biggest in-state football rivalry is the annual fall matchup between Michigan State University and the University of Michigan. It's a day when the blood pressure of fans reaches astronomical highs. The teams on the field are poised for contentious battle. It's the Spartans against the Wolverines. (Somehow this doesn't quite make sense . . . seems like a mighty warrior should be able to easily conquer a lowly weasel.)

What has come to be known as The Great Divide officially began in 1953, the year MSU entered the Big Ten.

In honor of this momentous occasion, then-Governor G. Mennen Williams donated a four-foot-high wooden statue of the mythical lumberjack character Paul Bunyan, wearing a cap, shirt, and blue-green pants. Straddling a map of the state, Bunyan's legs are spread wide with an ax plunked down between them. This massive and colorful structure was then riveted on to a five-foot-high base and would be presented to the winners by the governor. Not a pretty picture, and definitely not a lightweight. Michigan Coach Lloyd Carr (1995-2007) called it "the ugliest trophy in college football."

Frankly, the trophy was so ugly Michigan said they would refuse it if they won that first year. Not to worry: Michigan State beat them in East Lansing (14-6), and the Paul Bunyan–Governor of Michigan trophy remained there for the next twelve months, until the two teams met again.

The trophy has done a great deal of traveling between East Lansing and Ann Arbor, where it seems to be spending more time. Through 2011, Michigan has won it thirty-four times, MSU twenty-three, with two ties.

When the Bunyan trophy is in Ann Arbor, it sits in Schembechler Hall (www.goblue.com). When it's in East Lansing, it's on display (under glass) in the Skandalaris Center (www.msuspartans.com).

Paul Bunyan puffs out his wooden chest as his boots appear to be crushing both Ann Arbor and East Lansing.
ANDY DUBILL

Unlikely Cofounders

Who says religion and politics don't mix? Not many people are aware that the University of Michigan was cofounded in 1817 by a rather unlikely trio: Fr. Gabriel Richard, a Catholic priest, Rev. John Monteith, a Presbyterian minister, and August Brevoort Woodward, the first Chief Justice of the Michigan Territory (for whom Woodward Avenue is named). Originally located in Detroit, under the name Cathelepistemian (University of Michigania), it didn't move to Ann Arbor until 1841.

Michigan State University was the first land grant college in the nation, established in 1855 as State Agricultural College. It became co-ed in 1870, admitting ten women, followed that same year by the University of Michigan, which enrolled only one female. It didn't actually become MSU until January 1, 1964, when the word "agriculture" was dropped from its official name.

Two Heads Make Beautiful Music Together
Ann Arbor

Ah, the sweet roar of an elephant tusk trumpet is music to the ear, at least in India. And in Ann Arbor, where it's a member of the Stearns Collection, the largest assembly of musical instruments in North America.

But these aren't just your run-of-the-mill trumpets or drums. Every piece in the collection of 2,500 is a rare example of how people around the world view the art and science of sound.

Take, for instance, the nineteenth-century "little Tibetan drums"—which, upon closer inspection, reveal their true identity as two skulls tied together like coconuts, covered with animal skins. Shamans

The sharpest tongue at the University of Michigan sticks out at the music school, firing an arrow from this 1883 dragonhead buzzed-lip tromba.

believed that the spirit of the person remained tucked inside, waiting to be released by the hands of a capable musician.

Not every piece has the luridness of the cranium twosome or the thighbone trumpet. With greater aesthetic value is the floral porcelain violin from Germany circa 1309 or the taus, a peacock vina from India.

And some of the ideas presented are extremely practical. The Gregorian Chant Book is sized almost larger than life at four by five feet, so that a single copy sufficed for the whole choir . . . an automatic guarantee that everyone was on the same page. One section includes a picture of Mary that chanters would kiss, but after accumulating more than a hundred years of saliva, it was decided this wasn't the most becoming page to display.

Most of the instruments were originally in the private collection of Detroit businessman Frederick Stearns as a manifestation of his intellectual interests. Donated in 1899, portions are rotated frequently in the Earl V. Moore School of Music Building, University of Michigan North Campus, 1100 Baits Drive (off Broadway Street). It's open Monday through Friday, 10:00 a.m. to 5:00 p.m. Call (734) 936-2891. Free. Additional instruments are on display in the lower level of Hill Auditorium. Learn more at www.music.umich.edu/research/stearns-collection.

The Peaks and Valleys of Art
Ann Arbor

At the university, you're walking along North Campus near the engineering building when you see something curious in the courtyard. At first it appears to be simply lumpy terrain, or some form of crop circles, or a new version of outdoor checkers. But no, it's the Wave Field, an extraordinary earth sculpture by internationally acclaimed artist Maya Lin—creator of the Vietnam Veterans Memorial in Washington, D.C.— made entirely of soil covered with grass.

Commissioned as a memorial to former aerodynamics graduate François-Xavier Bagnoud, Lin was determined to make this piece unique. After an exhaustive study, the decision was made to model it after the three-dimensional wave pattern found on the open sea. Two years in the making, the ninety-by-ninety-foot-square artwork, consisting of grassy waves rising six feet from the natural ground, was formally dedicated on October 6, 1995.

Interaction with this monument is not only acceptable, but desirable. Some days you'll see a slew of students with books in hand, lying comfortably among the ripples of earth, quietly absorbed in the presence beneath them, perhaps experiencing their personal earth-bound version of a Carnival cruise. With that, Lin knows that her mission has been accomplished, giving scholars the opportunity to "explore, study, play, enjoy."

The Wave Field sits in a courtyard adjacent to the François-Xavier Bagnoud Engineering Building at 1320 Beal Avenue. For more information call (734) 764-3310.

Forget dusting. It's watering, raking, and weeding that maintain this $250,000 sculpture where students playfully dip into one of the fifty grassy waves.

★ ★

Blind as a Bat . . . Not!
Bloomfield Hills

On the one hand, Kim Williams appears to be a fairly typical, fast-paced working mother, devoted to her two children. On the other, she's quite atypical, with responsibilities for the daily care and feeding of nearly a hundred live bats.

When nature called some years ago, she listened and answered. One day at the wildlife center where she was employed as a fresh-out-of-college graduate with a degree in zoology, someone brought in what he thought was an injured vampire bat. It was practically love at first bite. Upon completion of her master's research project in "batology," the Organization for Bat Conservation was established, becoming the only venue in Michigan where the furry mammals exist in captivity. (No, they're not birds, although that wasn't scientifically acknowledged until 1920.)

As executive director, Williams's duties are so diverse it would make most people go batty. (I'm sorry, I couldn't resist.) One minute she's stringing swinging chains of watermelon, bananas, and whole heads of lettuce for the daily . . . er, nightly feeding and exercise. The next, it's the placement of frozen pig-bloodsicles, followed by preparation for one of the 1,000 outreach programs delivered annually, during which, inevitably, she's sprayed with bat urine.

Martha Stewart, a lover of bats, or depending on your point of view, an old one herself, has given Williams several shots at national TV fame, proclaiming the benefits of these nocturnal wonders. Did you realize a bat with a 3½-inch wingspan can consume 1,000 mosquitoes an hour, or that scientists developed birth control pills with the assistance of female bats? And surprising to most, bats have excellent eyesight. The author of fourteen books on her flying friends, the bat lady has the answer to everything you'd ever want to know and then some.

Milly Hill Mine, in the Upper Peninsula's copper country, hosts the largest colony of hibernating bats in the entire United States—which in some ways resembles the ultimate spa experience. Being the bigger eaters, female bats devour as much food as they can all summer long, achieving a more-than-pleasingly plump figure. Then they enter into their October hibernation period and, almost like clockwork, wake up exactly six months later . . . skinny! Where do I sign up?

The Bat Zone, home to more than one hundred bats from around the world, is on the site of the former nature center at Cranbrook Institute of Science, 39221 Woodward Avenue. It's open daily throughout the summer, with special Friday night programs. During the school year it's open Saturday and Sunday only with special events during holidays. Admission is $5, plus a museum entrance fee. For more information and hours, call (248) 645-3232 or visit www.bat conservation.org.

Kim Williams whispers to her batty friend to "spread your wings," while those in the background remain hung up on being camera-shy.

★ ★

Grown Boy's Toys on Steroids
Brighton

Ken Lingenfelter's love for the automobile is so strong that it seems he may have been born with motor oil in his blood. He can clearly remember when he was only four years old, standing on a '55 Chevy, being able to correctly identify every car that passed down the street. It wasn't long before he had the biggest Matchbox car collection of anyone he knew.

Today his passion has driven him to have one of the largest full-size auto collections in the country. His first acquisition was a '77 Corvette,

Does Ken Lingenfelter drive his 2008 Lamborghini Reventon at its top speed of 211 mph on Interstate 96?

* *

when he "didn't have two nickels to rub together." After developing a successful title insurance company, which he sold "at the right time," he now is the proud owner of over two hundred vehicles, most of which are housed in a 40,000-square-foot warehouse.

Lingenfelter doesn't like to just look at his cars. On any given day, you may see him driving his candy apple red Alfa Romeo, or his "seriously fast" 2007 Callaway C16, or his 1969 Camaro Z28, which still has the original window sticker of $4096.75. But then again it could be the 1987 Porsche, which goes 0-62 mph in 3.2 seconds, topping out at 215 mph. Originally, he designed his garage so that you "never have to move another car to drive one," but that didn't last long.

The day I was there he wowed the crowd by revving up his 2003 660 hp Enzo Ferrari, which he purchased from Ralph Lauren, producing sounds and smells unknown to most ears and noses.

Bugattis and Bricklins . . . they're all here plus so much more, neatly divided into three rooms: foreign exotics, Corvettes, and muscle cars. Asking Lingenfelter which is his favorite is like asking a parent which child he or she likes best. He did disclose he considers the crown jewels to be the Bugatti Veyron EB and the Lamborghini Reventon.

The Lingenfelter Collection on 7819 Locklin Drive in Brighton is open only for fundraisers, hosted roughly forty times a year. If you can't make it to one of those, you can capture much of the excitement by visiting www.thelingenfeltercollection.com. Call (248) 486-5342 for event dates and time. Then you'll be able to share the sentiments expressed by one satisfied visitor who said, "There are cars here I never thought I'd see in my lifetime."

Capturing a Breathtaking Moment
Dearborn

The rich and famous give and receive gifts much different from the knickknacks from friends most of us have sitting on shelves. Take, for instance, the largesse of Thomas Edison's son, Charles, who presented to Henry Ford his father's last breath in a test tube. As the famous

★ ★

inventor was passing on, a rack of eight tubes lay next to his bed, and when the final moment arrived, the attending physician was ordered to seal each with paraffin. Sure, it sounds wacky, but you can see for yourself what the not-so-fresh air of Edison looks like in the Henry Ford Museum.

Dubbed "Henry's attic," this world-class collection of memories contains endless hidden treasures to pique an assortment of interests.

Will the Real McCoy Please Stand Up?

Ask anyone about the Real McCoy and expect to hear answers like, "Wasn't that a television show from the 1960s with Walter Brennan?" or "That was the guy on Family Feud, Hatfields versus the McCoys."

To tell the truth, most people don't realize that there is a single individual associated with the "Real McCoy." Born Elijah McCoy in 1843, he grew up in Ypsilanti to become one of the foremost African-American inventors of all time, awarded the rights to fifty-seven patents. His prized self-regulating lubricator for steam engines became so popular that dozens of oily imitators tried infiltrating the market, prompting wise customers to question, "Is this the real McCoy?"—a phrase born and bred in Michigan that's gone on to become an authentic Webster's entry.

The "real" McCoy lubricator, patented on March 28, 1882, shares a portion of the Made in America exhibit at the Henry Ford Museum in Dearborn.

★ ★

A handwritten letter dated April 10, 1934, from Clyde Barrow—of the Bonnie and Clyde duo—thanks the automaker for the high quality of the V-8, handpicking the brand as his exclusive getaway car. "For sustained speed and freedom from trouble the Ford has got ever [*sic*] other car skinned." Expect to hear that endorsement in next year's Super Bowl commercial.

The museum and village together will take you back to another time through actual homes, shops, businesses, and, of course, Ford's personal gallery of gifts. Don't miss two of the more notorious exhibits: President Lincoln's theater chair the night he was shot and the limousine in which President Kennedy was assassinated.

Touring the Henry Ford Museum and Greenfield Village will satisfy every out-of-town guest for hours or days. Part of what is now called The Henry Ford, the museum is open year-round. Hours at the Village vary. Located at 20900 Oakwood, their web address is www.thehenry ford.org. Call (313) 982-6001. Admission is charged. Group tours are available. For information on the museum's IMAX Theatre, call (313) 271-1570.

Green Giant Sprouts Wings
Detroit

Ask anyone in the city, and he or she will tell you the Spirit of Detroit is hockey. To drive home that point, during the play-offs every year since 1997, the 26-foot bronze *Spirit of Detroit* sculpture, nicknamed Jolly Green Giant, turns a brighter shade of red, dressing up in his own Red Wings jersey.

Bob Phillips, vice president of East Side Team Sports in Warren, is the responsible party, "borrowing" the idea from the Philadelphia Flyers. He figured, "What the heck," imitation is the highest form of flattery, let's ease the burden of the *Spirit of Detroit,* who's been carrying around the weight of the world for decades, by turning him into the biggest Wings fan this town has ever seen.

Red Wings, Pistons, and Tigers . . . where are the Lions?

Former team captain Steve Yzerman, with his size 50 jersey (applied to a multiple of 5.5), became the fit model for the thirty-five yards of cloth, assembled in two days. That was the easy part.

Getting *Spirit* dressed was the nightmare. A metal statue has a hot temper in the blazing sun, gets a little slippery when wet, and is about as cooperative as a two-year-old when it comes to moving a muscle, but when two guys finally were able to tackle his head and arms they snapped him up just like a pair of Dr. Dentons. Only to have the shirt erroneously ripped off the next day by a building supervisor. Another fine example of the exemplary communication skills in city government.

After all that, the Red Wings did win the Stanley Cup that year, and the whole process was repeated in 1998, except for the building supervisor, who was probably transferred to Philadelphia.

That jersey may be the team's good luck charm—the Red Wings have been in the play-offs every year since. It worked for the Pistons, too. The team won an NBA championship in 2004 when *Spirit* wore their jersey. In 2006 he sported a Super Bowl XL shirt. Do you think it'll have the same effect on the Detroit Lions?

The *Spirit of Detroit,* dressed and undressed, sits on the west side of the Coleman A. Young municipal building (formerly known as the City County Building) at the foot of Woodward and Jefferson.

When the Brim Hits Your Eye . . . Hat's Amore
Detroit

Borsalino . . . Dobbs . . . Kangol . . . not a roll call at boot camp. Rather these are some of the head-toppers people have been buying at Henry the Hatter since 1893. Detroit's oldest retail establishment has moved a couple of times to make way for the city's new growth, settling in comfortably at its current location in 1952.

The one and only Henry was Henry Komrofsky. Today it's Paul Wasserman who's carrying on the fourth-generation tradition of fitting the heads of the city's well dressed.

Every Detroit mayor since the store first opened has walked out carrying a new chapeau in one of the coveted hatboxes.

So how do you make a living from a store filled with nothing but hats, save for the few umbrellas and canes? While you may not see men wearing a formal fedora every day, Wasserman credits his celebrated customers like Kid Rock, Jack White, Detroit Lion Dominic Raiola, and Lem Barney for keeping the fashion accessory out in the public eye. Okay, so the merchandise appears to be a bit sexist, unofficially labeled "for men only," but a number of women have been known to break through those barriers and come out looking as chic as anyone.

Obviously, business is good. With an additional location in Southfield, each year 10,000 hats (those with a brim) and 10,000 caps (those with a visor) find a new perch.

Wasserman, who will custom-design anything your head desires, managed to deflate the rumor behind President John F. Kennedy's inauguration. According to his version of the story, a silk top hat had been mailed to Kennedy, but when it was opened (at the last minute), it was discovered it was too small to wear comfortably the entire day. So sadly for the industry, it was the size of the noggin that gave all future presidents the nod to go hatless their first day in office.

Sizes at Henry the Hatter range from 6¾ to 8, with prices ranging $45 to $600. This Detroit institution has been recognized as a Centennial Business by the Historical Society of Michigan. It's located at 1307 Broadway, open Monday through Saturday. Call (313) 962-0970 or visit www.henrythehatterdetroit.com.

Beware of the Two-Headed Bookworm
Detroit

This place should come with a warning: Bibliophiles may find the contents habit forming. With more than a million titles, John K. King Used and Rare Books has been satisfying the public's hunger for the printed word since 1965. Once inside the main building, you can easily lose yourself for hours combing through thirty thousand square feet of shelves and shelves of books on every topic imaginable. It's all highly organized, and the staff is extremely helpful if you should be in need of direction.

A book about founder and owner John King could easily fill volumes. Defining himself as "the legendary two-headed bookworm," he was bitten by the literary bug in high school. He found his way into the business world shortly afterward. In 1983 he purchased his own building, which has quite a history itself. Originally the Advance Glove Factory Building, rumors have been around that one day in 1949, the employee-filled edifice was literally picked up and moved to make room for the impending freeway! King swears it's true, adding he has the confirming photographs locked safely away.

King has become a master at instantly recognizing the value of any tome. Using his "sixth sense" and a relatively simple equation, based on supply and demand, he personally assesses each item. Recently baby boomers have driven up the price of Dick and Jane readers, which were never allowed outside the classroom. Thanks to the nostalgia trend, the primers are selling now for anywhere between $40 and $100.

Some of the more valuable "finds" are next door in the former Otis Elevator Building. Larger than its neighbor at fifty thousand square feet, the rare-book room has a museum-like quality, hosting myriad signed, first-edition pieces from the likes of Babe Ruth and John F. Kennedy. It's here that you'll also find the collection's oldest printed book: a Bible from 1491.

Prices of all works range from "free" (you'll always find a box of gratis goodies sitting at the front door) to "up to the stratosphere."

John K. King Used and Rare Books is located at 901 West Lafayette Boulevard in downtown Detroit. Open Monday through Saturday. Call (313) 961-0622 or visit www.rarebooklink.com. He's added two other locations recently: on the campus of Wayne State University, 5911 Case Avenue, Detroit, and 22524 Woodward Avenue in Ferndale (open Sunday, too).

★ ★

Past and Present Dancin' in the Streets
Detroit

As a kid, Jerome Meriweather lived across the street from 2648 West Grand Boulevard and watched inquisitively as three teenage girls and a middle-age woman would get in and out of a limo for hours, without ever going anywhere. Later he came to appreciate the girls as the Supremes and the woman as Maxine Powell, their etiquette coach, teaching them how in ladylike fashion to enter and exit the vehicle in a miniskirt.

RESIDENT GRIOT—a tribal historian—is the title on Jerome's cap nowadays, as he stands inside the famous address on Hitsville, USA, home to the Motown Museum. If the walls could talk, they'd resonate with the same stories he's sharing about the music industry phenomenon of the 1960s, founded by Berry Gordy Jr. with an $800 loan.

This stucco two-story studio where Gordy resided was in operation twenty-four hours a day seven days a week, turning out hit after hit from young Detroiters like Smokey Robinson, Stevie Wonder, and Diana Ross, who all did double duty as record packers and restroom cleaners.

Everything inside is open for the public's perusal, left exactly the way it was, with flooring worn out by dancing feet and piano keyboards marked with stickers for artists who couldn't read music. Polish and pizzazz show up in the representative costumes . . . Michael Jackson's black fedora and white sequined (right hand only) glove and the Supremes' splashy sequined gowns, each weighing in at an astounding thirty-two pounds. No wonder they were all so thin—you couldn't help but lose weight carrying that extra baggage.

There's even an opportunity to try out your voice in the famed echo chamber, guaranteed to make anyone sound good. Don't get your hopes up for a recording contract, though. Motown headed to California in 1972, and was eventually sold for $61 million. Even though Gordy still maintains a home on Boston Boulevard, he's not around to put your record to the lunch test . . . where he'd ask random citizens if they'd prefer to spend their money on the music or a sandwich. If the song got one sandwich vote, it was never released.

Definitely worth a trip to "Stop in the Name of Love" of Motown memories, the Motown Historical Museum is open Tuesday through Saturday, plus Monday during the months of July and August. Tours leave at regular intervals. The address hasn't changed—2648 West Grand Boulevard; (313) 875-2264. Visit the museum online at www .motownmuseum.com.

No Refuse Refused

Detroit

A trip down Heidelberg Street is like entering the Disney World of recyclables. Tires, shoes, vacuum cleaners, street signs, broken dolls, cardboard taxis . . . all strewn across lawns or hanging from trees. Houses, adorned with so much old junk you can't make out the windows from the doors. Despite all this, there's a sense of whimsy that appears to have artistically awakened an otherwise tired neighborhood.

That was the objective of artist Tyree Guyton when he created the Heidelberg Project in 1986, only to be met with acrimonious assaults from local politicians, claiming it wasn't art at all, but just an unorganized heap of trash. Five years later city officials sprang a surprise attack, bulldozing four of Guyton's bedazzled homes.

Perseverance paid off, and today the project stands as garish as ever. For a picturesque pick-me-up, polka dots permeate almost everything paintable. Inspired by his grandfather's love of jelly beans, Guyton started out painting the dots on houses, then trees, then the pavement, "and I wish I could polka dot all the people, too."

In cooperation with a local elementary school, Guyton educates young people in his style of "street art," pleased to see that the block he grew up on is stamped, hopefully for a long time to come, with his personal trademark.

The city calls it junk; the owner calls it art. The mouse atop
the OJ House (obstruction of justice) concludes it's a toss up.

To celebrate their twenty-fifth anniversary in 2011, twenty-five
painted car hoods were placed all over town saying, "What's good in
your hood?" or "Home is where the art is."

The Heidelberg Project is free of charge and gets more than
275,000 visitors a year. It's located on Heidelberg Street on Detroit's
East Side between Elery and McDougall; a detailed map is accessible
through their website: www.heidelberg.org. For other inquiries call
(313) 974-6896.

A Feather You Can Bowl Over

Detroit

Here's a solution for the sports fan who has trouble deciding whether to spend a few hours involved in a tantalizing game of shuffleboard, bocce ball, or horseshoes. Try feather bowling, a unique fusion of all three that arrived in Detroit with Belgian immigrants during Prohibition. It takes the worry out of breaking a nail on traditional bowling balls.

The playing field is a seventy-foot concave trough, or alley, covered with an appealing mixture of dirt and ox blood. (Not as gross as it sounds, bearing a close resemblance to tightly packed sawdust.) Each

In almost one hundred years the only thing that's changed on these bowling lanes is the feather.

participant takes a three-and-a-quarter-pound wooden ball having an imagined similitude to dinosaur dung and whirls it down, watching it traverse the lane on its way to the upright feather waiting at either end. Closest to the tickler scores a point. Ten points and your team claims victory.

The Cadieux Cafe is the only place in the country where feather bowlers can hang out. Not á thing has changed on the pair of lanes that have been here since 1929, not even the faithful league members who show up every night during the week for a game of three-on-three. Participants say, "Drinking doesn't hurt the camaraderie either."

The Belgian influence extends to the beer—described as "funky"—and the food. Well known for its mussels, once a Friday-only item, Cadieux currently makes them available daily, although connoisseurs say for the best flavor, eat them only in months containing the letter *R*.

A pleasurable party activity, feather bowling lanes are available for rent—$25 an hour weekdays, $40 weekends. Cadieux Cafe has occupied the corner at 4300 Cadieux for almost a hundred years. Call (313) 882-8560 or visit www.cadieuxcafe.com.

In 2000 Bath City Bistroin Mount Clemens opened three feather bowling lanes, which they call trough bowling, but they're covered with a compressed rubber padding. The health department said no to the plasma–dirt and food combo . . . Cadieux Cafe's age kept it grandfathered. The Bistro—which has had its plumage pushed around by Pamela Anderson and Kid Rock—rents lanes by the hour also. Find it at 75 Macomb Place (586-469-0917) or visit www.bathcitybistro.com.

Woodward Dream Cruise
Detroit Area

Detroiters still refer to themselves as East Siders and West Siders, with Woodward Avenue as the dividing line. Compared to these allegiances, Jerusalem is one big happy family.

Every August, however, the same street that divides Detroiters also brings them together for an event called the Woodward Dream Cruise.

★ ★

It's the world's longest, largest, and loudest free automotive event, with more than 40,000 custom cars, hot rods, muscle cars, and antiques cruising up and down Woodward Avenue through eight cities. Add the music, food, and crowds, and it "ain't nothin' but a party."

Where else but Detroit would 2.5 million people line a street to watch cars drive by? Charles Brady King would probably roll over in his grave. He reportedly drove the first automobile down Woodward in 1896. But the inspiration for the Woodward Dream Cruise has a more recent history.

In the 1950s, the eight-lane road tempted young men fueled by cheap gas and testosterone poisoning to bring their wheels to Woodward to do a little cruising. There was no better way to impress the bouffant-haired, poodle-skirted ladies at drive-in restaurants like Ted's and The Totem Pole. The hottest of the hot rods competed on Woodward in an attempt to become king of the road. Legend has it that the Big Three tested their top-secret project cars many a night after dark on Woodward.

The godfather of the Woodward Dream Cruise was Nelson House, a man looking for a way to raise funds for a kids' soccer field. He and a group of volunteers launched the nostalgic Woodward Dream Cruise. What was supposed to be a onetime event became an annual trip in a time machine. Although technically the Cruise takes place on the third Saturday in August, car enthusiasts bring out their chariots to get in the mood for an entire week.

Nearly one hundred local charities in the eight host cities of Berkley, Bloomfield Hills, Bloomfield Township, Ferndale, Huntington Woods, Pleasant Ridge, Pontiac, and Royal Oak all benefit from the sale of official merchandise and refreshments sold at the Woodward Dream Cruise. The cruise generates more than $56 million each year for the Metro Detroit economy, but, more important, it gives middle-age men the chance to remember the two things they miss from their youth: horsepower and hair. For information visit www.woodwarddream cruise.com.

★ ★

Mr. Unordinary
Farmington Hills

As I approach the entrance to Marvin's Marvelous Mechanical Museum, the nine-foot clock overhead says I'm two hours late for my appointment. How could that be? A second glance provides the answer: The timepiece is running backward, with all numbers and hands going counterclockwise, a tip-off to the antics inside.

The Polish Muslims

There aren't many bands that would begin the PR blurb on the back of their CD with "A few short decades ago, the Polish Muslims were only known to patrons of after hours rave parties and penitentiary inmates."

But the Polish Muslims aren't just any band. If Lawrence Welk and Tina Turner had a child and it was adopted by Sly and the Family Stone and Monty Python, you still wouldn't have all of the nuances they put into their music. As Dave Uhalick puts it, "Our music is just, well, it's none of your business what our music is."

The eight-member band is a mainstay in the Detroit area, playing gigs for anybody who wants an instant party with their "polka 'n' roll." Although the idea of a polka beat dropped in periodically along with an accordion solo in the middle of a rock classic like "Dance to the Music" may take some getting used to, fans of the band have done just that. The band's concerts are a cross between a mosh pit and a Polish wedding.

The lyrics to their songs rest strongly on their Detroit roots and include so many references to the area that you need a Detroit

★ ★

Showers of neon splash everywhere, and among several busloads of keyed-up kids, I spot owner Marvin Yagoda, who's playing hooky from his day job. A full-time pharmacist, his animatronics apparatus "museum" is the result of "a hobby that got out of hand." It's filled with a hodgepodge of coin-operated machines—no count on how many, but all 1,000 electrical outlets are in full use—from a 1923 motorized fortune-teller to a series of high-tech video WaveRunners.

dictionary to translate. Their second CD—titled, appropriately enough, *The Polish Muslims Make #2*—features a cover festooned with more local photographs than a chamber of commerce brochure. Song titles like "Where Hamtramck Is" (sung to the tune of "Where the Action Is") and "Paczki Day" (to the tune of "Yesterday") mean very little to anyone who doesn't know that Hamtramck is a working-class Polish enclave and a paczki (pronounced poonch-key) is a jelly doughnut, served the Tuesday before Ash Wednesday, with the density of a paperweight.

The surprising thing is the band is becoming much more than a local phenomenon, drawing crowds all across the Midwest at places that wouldn't know a paczki from a pizza. Their name alone has made them a favorite at Polish festivals, although they make a point of explaining the group isn't your typical polka band. They're more your typical "Rock 'n' Roll Out the Barrel" polka band.

And when it comes to competition . . . What competition?

Check out their latest CD, *Polk-a Fun at Christmas*, and other good stuff at www.thepolishmuslims.com.

Pharmacist Marvin Yagoda's vintage carousel administers a dose of good medicine to happy kids.

Yagoda is the Willy Wonka of electromechanical gizmos. At one point he gathers a crowd to watch Marvallo the Buffalo lose his temper, when billows of smoke spew from the animal's nostrils. Next, a young lady is beckoned over to the counter where a sign cautions danger of high winds. Riotous laughs break out as a breeze blows up her legs.

With fifty airplanes circling the ceiling in conveyor-belt fashion, I can barely hear when Yagoda tells me he's quenching the public's thirst for anything involving love and torture. Passing by the "Love Pilot"—which, for a quarter, promises to "steer you straight" (a much different meaning in the 1920s)—to instead pay fifty cents to watch an electrocution, it soon becomes apparent that agonizing pain is the hands-down favorite.

I choose to drop my last coin on the "Most Disgusting Spectacle" as a handful of anxious third-graders stand by starry-eyed. The mannequin resting inside begins to move one hand, prompting us to all shriek a nauseated "ooh," followed by a chorus of outrageously silly giggles. I walk away confident my money was well spent.

Marvin's Marvelous Mechanical Museum is the right prescription for fun at any age. Located in the back of a strip mall at 31005 Orchard Lake Road, all 5,500 square feet are open seven days a week, 365 days a year. Call (248) 626-5020 or log on to www.marvin3m.com. Free to get in, but load up on quarters. Refreshments available.

La Blanchisserie Francaise . . . un Bon Endroit a Manger*
Fenton

Ask any food critic worth his or her salt for the name of the best restaurant in the country and they'll promptly identify The French Laundry. The question becomes, which one are they referring to? The restaurant in Napa Valley, California, where the cheapest meal is $150, or the one in Fenton where you can order one of sixty gourmet sand-wiches with inventive names like "Marionette and the Bust of Elvis" and "The Floydian Slip"?

The year was 1997. Mark Hamel, coming from a family of restaura-teurs, didn't set out to copy the name when he opened his own place in a 1932 building, formerly the site of a family laundry. He was look-ing for a suitable "blue-collar name" when the answer befell him: The French Laundry. *C'est magnifique!*

What started out as a major challenge, trying to outfit the restau-rant's 1,300 square feet on a limited budget, has now become its trademark. Furnished with other people's throwaways, nothing inside the restaurant matches. An eclectic mix of 1950s metal and wooden tables and chairs graces the newly expanded 2,600 square feet, with seating for 135. People drop off things from their grandmother's attic, like the vintage refrigerator adorning the main dining room.

Mais, oui! After experiencing it, you'll agree "The French Laundry . . . a good place to eat."

This French laundry prides itself on pressed garlic, steamed vegetables, and an eclectic array of furnishings.
MARY NOWAK

While the decor is kooky, the food is divine. And you can view every morsel being prepared in the glassed-in kitchen, even the labor-intensive pies, rolling out the door at a pace of three hundred per day during Christmas season. All fruit pies are made on premises, with a rotating repertoire of more than twenty mouth-watering varieties.

Specialty dinners are scheduled throughout the year, offering diners the chance to learn about and experience newfangled dishes in a novel setting. Bastille Day is a major holiday here, celebrating the 1984 victory of the first woman to ever win the Tour de France, Fenton's own Marinne Martin.

Draggin' Lake Orion for Monsters

There are a million reasons behind the acquisition of high school mascots.

Practicality bred the Dearborn Fordson Tractors, named for the nearby Ford tractor plant. In Bad Axe, it seems logical the Hatchets take the field. But there's quite a story behind the Lake Orion High School Dragons.

It all started back in 1894 when several ladies, on a leisurely cruise in their rowboat, reported spotting a real dragon vaulting its ugly head out of the water. The town was horrified, and for several years the account kept everyone on shore.

With numerous sightings, the frightful tale steadily grew. The monster once was believed to have been at least eighty feet long, devouring everything in its path including cows that had gone astray.

Alas, there was a happy ending to the yarn when the elusive creature was identified as a set of rims from wagon wheel pulleys that a young lad had covered with canvas and anchored in the lake. With the truthful discovery, the suggestion was made that the ladies of Lake Orion in the future restrict their drinking to well water.

The chic charm of the French Laundry spills out into the rest of Dibbleville, the downtown section of Fenton founded in 1834 by Clark Dibble. A stroll through some of the quaint shops, such as The Iron Grate, Yesterday's Treasures, Sweet Variations, and Mimi and Lola's, can help burn off any potential "pie pounds."

Open seven days a week for breakfast, lunch, and dinner. Located in the heart of Fenton at 125 West Shiawassee, call (810) 629-8852 or visit www.lunchandbeyond.com.

Custer Still Stands

People in Monroe refer to Steve Alexander as the "guy who portrays General Custer." Spend some time talking to him and you'll walk away convinced there's a stronger power seeded within.

First, there's the striking natural resemblance to the famous general. While he's on the job as a surveyor, strangers habitually stop and ask, "Did anyone ever tell you that you look exactly like General Custer?" Okay, so the physical similarity could be a fluke.

Alexander was also an accomplished reader at an extremely early age. Before long "General Custer's thoughts had found a place inside a three-year-old boy." Obsessed with his hero throughout his school years, his book report topics never strayed. A check on his personal library shelves today reveals more than 1,000 books on George Armstrong Custer. All happenstance?

A stop at Montana's Big Horn Museum in 1986 to go to the bathroom, the fulfillment of a lifelong dream (not the bathroom part), proved to be a critical turning point. Dressed in his customary cowboy boots and a buckskin jacket purchased at a garage sale, Alexander fell into the path of Diana Scheidt, organizer of the Big Horn reenactment, who claimed she had been searching for "the man who knows more about Custer than Custer knew about himself." No training required, he immediately fell into uniform, diffusing Custer's persona. Merely being in the right place at the right time?

Contrary to signs along Interstate 75, Monroe is not the general's hometown; his birthplace was New Rumley, Ohio, which has taken Alexander under its wing, naming him the city's official General Custer. Lectures across the country, movie and television appearances, including *Encounters with the Unexplained*, searching for the accurate story of the general's death (theories say he was humiliatingly smothered by a three-hundred-pound woman), and a string of reenactments keep Alexander away from home forty-eight weekends

Mirror images: Is that General George Custer
or Monroe's Steve Alexander?

ROGER HOFFMAN

a year. Or at least they did until he got busy restoring the house he
recently purchased—the very home George and Libbie Custer lived in
together during the 1800s.

Maybe it's all just a coincidence. Maybe not. Either way, Steve
Alexander never complains about "becoming my childhood dream."

You can contact Alexander by e-mail at custergac@aol.com or
check out his website at www.georgecuster.com.

★ ★

Make Mine Marsh Rabbit
Monroe

The focus of this highly coveted culinary experience isn't a meal from
Emeril, but rather an opportunity to experience a two-hundred-year-
old cultural tradition of savoring the wintertime delicacy commonly
known as . . . muskrat. Each January and February dozens of churches,
VFW halls, and private clubs in Monroe host bountiful banquets with
the little furry rodent as the main event. (The fur is gone; a number of
small bones remain.) Credit goes to the French settlers, who were so
fervent in their taste for muskrat that they requested and received special dispensation from the church to allow its consumption on Fridays.

A strict vegetarian, the marsh rabbit—as they call it here—has been
reported to be one of the cleanest animals around, if not the cheapest. At last check the critters, any size you want, were going for a buck
apiece.

So don't knock it till you've tried it, and those who have say an
incomparably sweet, buttery flavor has even the biggest skeptics coming back for seconds. Of course, it's all in the preparation. Localites
favor the rich "so-dark-it's-almost-black" meat parboiled in wine with
carrots and onions, topped with a creamed corn gravy.

VFW Post 3295 in Erie hosts an annual muskrat dinner complete
with banana peppers, mashed potatoes, creamed corn, and turtle
soup. (You supply the Pepto Bismol.) Call (734) 848-8091.

The Monroe County Historical Museum can fill you in on other 'rat
munchings. Contact them at (734) 240-7780.

The Hunt for Big Foot Ends Here
Plymouth

Whoever coined the expression "size really doesn't matter" probably
never met Robert Wadlow, the world's tallest man. Born on February
22, 1918, at a normal eight and a half pounds, a pituitary gland disor-
der sprouted him to 6' 2" and 195 pounds by the time he was eight.
As an adult, he grew to 8' 10½", with a size 37 shoe.

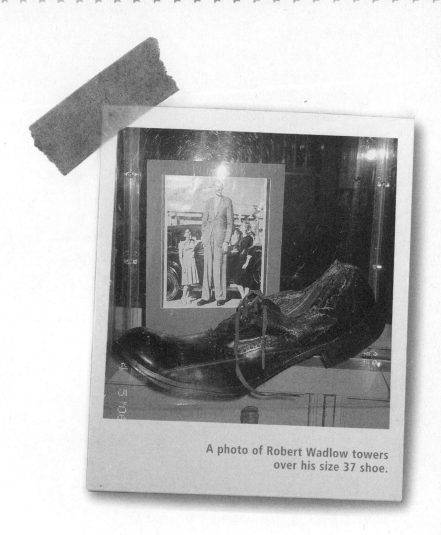

A photo of Robert Wadlow towers over his size 37 shoe.

It's that shoe, showcased in the Plymouth Historical Museum, that attracts the most oohs and ahs from young people. Why is it here? In the 1930s, Wadlow made a personal appearance in Plymouth promoting the Walkover Shoe Company, which custom made all his footwear. And he took his last step in Michigan, passing away in Manistee on July 15, 1940.

Another person who has filled big shoes is featured prominently in the museum, which houses the largest collection of Abraham Lincoln memorabilia in the state. Thanks to a donation from Dr. Weldon Petz, you can get up close and personal with the last lock of Lincoln's hair, cut from his wound on the night of his assassination by the man who performed his autopsy, Surgeon General Barnes. Thousands of other Lincoln items sit here in Plymouth, home to the Civil War's 24th Company C, which suffered devastating losses at the Battle of Gettysburg.

Few people may realize that, at one time, Plymouth was the BB Gun Capital of the World. The BB gun was invented and initially produced here in 1886. Ninety percent of the world's BB guns were made in Plymouth until 1958, when the Daisy Air Rifle Company moved out of town. An entire room of air rifles is set up exactly as it was more than a hundred years ago. Everything in it is authentic, except for the floor. It's now covered with polyurethane to stop visitors from picking out all the BBs.

The Plymouth Historical Museum also hosts special exhibits throughout the year, where you may see the world's smallest set of dominoes or an assortment of vintage Santa dolls. Owned and operated by the Plymouth Historical Society, it's open Wednesday, Friday, Saturday, and Sunday, 1:00 to 4:00 p.m. at 155 South Main Street (aka the Dunning Memorial Building). When you're in the Lincoln exhibit, be sure to ask for historian Fred Priebe . . . you'll think you're staring into the eyes of Abe himself . . . honest. For more information call (734) 455-8940 or visit www.plymouthhistory.org. Fee.

In This Place Size Really Does Matter
Southgate

Wow! What a whopper! Well, not exactly. It is a burger, but it happens to be the biggest burger ever seen on the face of the planet. The *Guinness Book of World Records* says so, too.

Mallie's Sports Grill has garnered a whale of a reputation for doing things on a grand scale. A quick glance at the menu and your eyes are drawn to their ten-pound "Monster burger," which requires forty-five minutes to prepare. Both the fifty-pound "Behemoth burger" and the

A flying saucer or a soaring burger?

one-hundred-pound "Goliath burger" need to be ordered forty-eight hours in advance.

Then there's the "Absolutely Ridiculous burger." It's called that because, at 320 pounds, "there is absolutely no reason for this burger." Three people work together to flip it; seventy-two hours' notice is required.

Owner Steve Mallie set his sights high when he first opened the doors in 2005. Just three years later, he went for his first *Guinness* record with a 134-pound burger, standing about two feet tall, measuring twenty-six inches across and commanding eight hours of baking time.

Each year since, they raise they own bar with new *Guinness* records of 164.8 pounds, then 185.6 pounds, until 2011 when they topped out at 319 pounds.

All this beefy news hasn't gone unnoticed. In 2009, Adam Richman, host of the Travel Channel's *Man vs. Food,* taped a segment at Mallie's in an attempt to consume a 190-pound burger in two hours or less. Chowing down with a team of forty people, they only managed to scarf 160 pounds before time ran out. The bodacious burgers have also been featured, not surprisingly, on *Modern Marvels* on the History Channel and *Outrageous Food* on the Food Network.

It's Not Easy Being Green

The thought of millions of worms crawling around at their workplace would probably make most people shudder. But for the employees of DMF Bait Company, it's a sign that business is good. The more creepy crawlers there are, the better they like it.

The first larva leeched on in 1977, and ever since the number of creatures entering the building has risen dramatically; now the company can boast of 119 million Canadian nightcrawlers passing through their doors. That makes them the largest wholesale bait distributor in the world. Worm searching at Wal-Mart? You'll find them . . . the chain is their No. 1 customer. DMF has now sold over 2.2 billion worms and in 2009 built a 7,000-square-foot cooler that stores thirty million of the wiggly creatures.

In case you're still hungry, consider trying the "Ginormous" twenty-inch chocolate chip cookie with sprinkles. Or maybe you'd prefer the "Colossal Sundae," where one and a half gallons of ice cream meets toppings and whipped cream.

There's seating for 190, who can watch their favorite sport on one of thirty-six TVs, most of them big-screen with individual-size TVs in the booths.

Mallie's Sports Grill is at 19400 Northline Road in Southgate. Call (734) 287-0800 for current hours, or check out www.malliessportsgrill .com. Just in case you were wondering, they do sell fifteen to twenty of the ten-pound burgers every week.

And not all worms leave looking the same way as they came in: 2.1 million undergo a makeover that leaves them green. Not just any green, but a kryptonite-looking green. Chris Fry, inventory manager, says they get more repeat customers for their green worms than anything else. Apparently some people think the green ones give off an odor that the fish find exceptionally attractive. What's in the green dye that causes fish to bite? Fry's lips are sealed, saying, "It's a trade secret."

DMF is strictly a wholesale operation, but know that when you hook up the next wiggler, he's most likely been here in Waterford. The company motto says it all: "Our worms catch fish or die trying." Visit DMF online at www.dmfbait.com for some fun facts. Did you know that night crawlers have five hearts? And although they are only a third of an ounce, they can move sixty times their own weight?

★ ★

Hips, Poodle Skirts, and Blue Suede Shoes
Ypsilanti

Elvis is alive and well and living in downtown Ypsilanti, at least for two days every July. What began as a Ladies Night Out event in 2000 with one Elvis doing karaoke has now turned into a major festival, officially sanctioned by Elvis Presley Enterprises.

The minute you drive into Depot Town, you'll notice evidence of the King. In the window of Fantasy Attic Costumes, there's an Elvis mannequin sporting his renowned jumpsuit, enticing wannabes to rent their own tight-fitting bodysuit and waterfall wig.

The Elvisfest crowd has a "hunk of burning love" for their idol.

The real action takes place in Riverside Park, where thousands of true-blue fans come from all over the Midwest to worship their idol. A huge stage is set up for professional Elvis tribute artists (don't call them impersonators) to strut across and wow the hysterical crowds with their musical gyrations. The women swoon and scream, some even tossing flowers on stage. At one point "Elvis" yells out, "Boy, it's hot up here" and then rips off his scarf and throws it out to the frenzied mosh-pit-like audience. They're convinced they're witnessing the reincarnation of the real thing. One year a woman jumped on stage, pounced on top of Elvis, and wouldn't leave until security was called to physically remove her.

The dozen or so tribute artists represent all phases of the King's life. You'll see a fat Elvis, a skinny one, versions young and old, and everything in between. (Rumors were circulating that some went so far as to have had plastic surgery enhancements.)

Vendors will satisfy your appetite for any type of Elvis memorabilia your heart could ever desire. Whip out that charge card and you could be the proud owner of an Elvis beach towel, purse, earrings, magnet, or a key chain with a photocopy of Elvis' 21st birthday driver's license when it said he was 170 pounds.

Elvisfest MI is a nonprofit organization located at 106 W. Michigan Avenue. Call (734) 480-3974, ext. 2, for more information. To really get "All Shook Up," check out their fun-filled website at www.mielvisfest .org. Admission to the festival is $15 on Friday (5:00 p.m. to midnight), $20 on Saturday (noon to midnight). Children twelve and under are free.

A Cow Who's a Star on Facebook

Ypsilanti

A cow with its own Facebook page? Yep, it's true, but considering how long the cow has been continuously standing it might not be so surprising.

Known simply as The Cow, she's had her hooves firmly planted on the roof of the Carry Dairy since 1966. The business is even older than she is, having started in 1962 and still going strong.

The "One Way" sign must be hung so only the cow can read it.

Carry Dairy was originally co-owned by two former milk delivery men who, after four years, were looking for ways to increase their business. Enter someone on his way to Wisconsin with a fifteen-foot-high cow in his truck. At that height The Cow was tough to miss. An offer was made and accepted, ending her traveling days forever. How anybody got all 2,500 pounds of her inflexible body up on the roof without injuring his or her own body remains a mystery.

Seemingly happy and content, The Cow beckons customers to the small store with two drive-up windows, one in the front, one in the back. Patrons pull up their cars, a clerk runs to their vehicle, takes their order, hustles back inside to gather the goods, and brings their packages, all under the keen eye, or derriere, of The Cow.

Ninety-five percent of their business is conducted via carry-out. People still buy milk, but the biggest seller is lottery tickets. Those with enough energy to come inside will find an assortment of just about everything you'd see in a typical convenience store. In the coolers lining the back wall, I even spotted a chilled bottle of Boone's Farm Watermelon Wine, restoring some fond memories from my college days.

At last count The Cow had nearly 5,000 Facebook fans who fill her wall with remembrances of days gone by, when perhaps they used to buy beer at night with a difficult-to-decipher fake ID.

Carry Dairy is located at 979 Ecorse Road. Hours are Monday through Friday 8:30 a.m. to 9:00 p.m., Saturday 9:00 a.m. to 9:00 p.m., and Sunday 10:00 a.m. to 8:00 p.m. The phone number is (734) 483-5648.

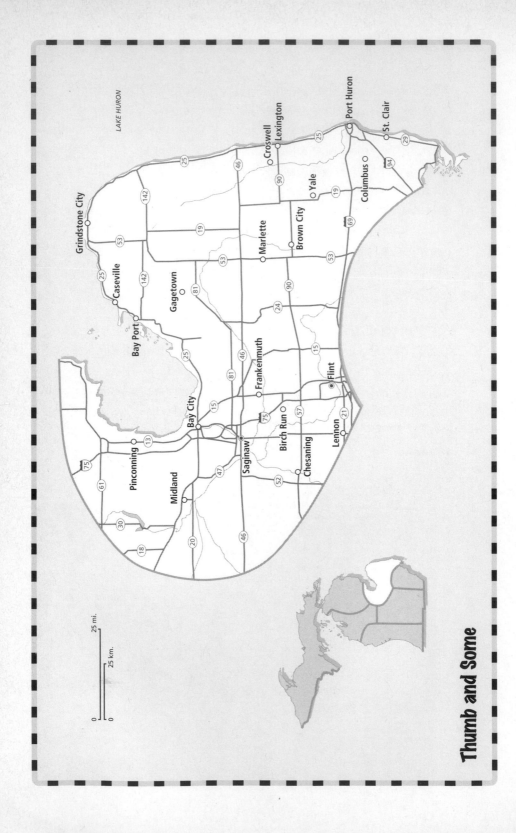

LAKE HURON

Grindstone City

Caseville

Bay Port

Pinconning

Midland

Bay City

Saginaw

Gagetown

Frankenmuth

Birch Run

Chesaning

Lennon

Flint

Marlette

Brown City

Croswell

Lexington

Yale

Columbus

Port Huron

St. Clair

25 mi.

25 km.

Thumb and Some

2

Thumb and Some

When someone gives a "thumbs up," it's the universal sign for "A-OK," "That's it," "You done good." The region included in Michigan's thumb certainly exemplifies all of those . . . giving an outward sign of approval of our state for the rest of the world to see.

We'd like to share a thumbnail sketch of our far east, where countryside meets 150 miles of lakeshore. It's a top-producing area for dry beans (Michigan is second in the nation), corn, and sugar beets (Michigan is fifth in the United States in sweetness from the ground, first in sweetness of disposition of its population). Bound by Lake Huron, here you can hold vigil for the numerous fish—salmon are among the best thumb suckers—and international freighters as they pass up and down the St. Lawrence Seaway.

The thumb is one of three Michigan points connecting to a foreign country, with the 1938 opening of the Blue Water Bridge linking Port Huron to Sarnia, Canada.

And now some rules of thumb:

- *Wear comfortable shoes*
  - — to promenade the longest freshwater boardwalk in America in St. Clair.
  - — to walk on the natural breakwall in Grindstone City, made of broken grindstones, or the 4,750-pound Grindstone Memorial at the corner of Copeland and Rouse.

— to climb the ninety-four steps of Michigan's oldest lighthouse at Fort Gratiot in Port Huron.

- Keep your head up and eyes open when traveling through Marlette and Brown City, both known for UFO sightings.
- Head to Bay Port, the village where the fish caught the man, at least once in your life the first weekend in August for Bay Port Fish Sandwich Days to sample their secret-recipe two-fisted fish sandwich.
- Keep an open mind as you thumb through the other curiosities of this section.

Ghosts, Legends, and Table 14
Bay City

Ghost sightings are so plentiful in Bay City, Casper should become the area's official mascot. Tales of debauchery gush out of historical publications. But a fix is close at hand for the hordes of inquiring minds who want to know more about the wicked ways that once existed here. The Ghost, Legends, and Lore Tour begins smack dab in the middle of "Hell's Half Mile" (once filled with 147 saloons) and doesn't stop until you've been through a dozen of the city's most popular haunts.

Michiganians love their Paul Bunyan. The fabled lumberjack is believed to have been modeled after Joe Fournier, whose ghost has been roaming the upper halls of The Campbell House since the time of his murder there in 1875.

Simmons Jewelers feels the presence of Orville, a worker who years ago refused to be fired. One female employee was convinced of Orville's ghostly spirit when he left a dusty handprint on her behind.

The granddaddy of them all is Old City Hall, with two jail cells in the basement and two phantoms casting a "creepy aura" on the restaurant inside. First thing every morning, manager Rose Grappin heads over to examine Table 14. She swears the bits of coal she finds are the ghost's nightly deposit.

Old City Hall Restaurant, 814 Saginaw Street, is open Monday through Saturday. Closed Sunday. Call ahead for Table 14: (989) 892-4140.

★ ★

Head Over Heels in Love

Bay City

When Bay City schoolteacher Anna Edson Taylor fell for a man, she fell so hard . . . well, hard enough to go right to the front page of the record books as the first person to successfully barrel over Niagara Falls. Allowing herself to be strapped into a cushion-lined barrel made expressly to her specifications by the West Bay City Cooperage Company, Taylor was going to find fame, fortune, and a trip to the altar with her fifty-year-old lover.

On October 24, 1901, her sixty-third birthday (although she'd led everyone, even her boyfriend, to believe she was forty-three), the barrel was given a heave-ho for a raucous seventeen-minute ride down the rapids of the Horseshoe Falls. Upon retrieving it, the few observers present were shocked to find her alive, without a single broken bone, and able to convey clearly her profound words of wisdom: "No one ought ever do that again."

Sadly, there were no offers for athletic endorsements, no book deals. Nor did any proposals for marriage materialize. Taylor died twenty years later, brokenhearted, penniless, and buried in a pauper's grave in Niagara Falls, New York.

More than fifty years went by before the Bay City Chamber of Commerce committed to changing the status of this daredevil's unrecognizable name by bringing her body home for a more dignified burial. Any feisty old broad who subtracts twenty years from her age, and gets away with it, indubitably deserves better.

But two sides butted heads in court: the city and the Annie Taylor Preservation Society, who fought desperately to keep her remains in New York. After months of legal haggling, it was learned that Annie had left no lineage to approve the transfer, forcing the issue out of the halls of justice.

An Annie Edson Taylor memorial in Bay City's Veterans Memorial Park has been bantered about, but no final approval has yet been stamped on the proposed waterfall sculpture.

Tony's Grill, Tony's Grill is the place we pick
'Cuz we know, while we're there, we'll eat so much, we're sick.

Tony's I-75 is in Birch Run (exit 136) on 8781 Main Street. Call (989) 624-5860. Open every day at 6:00 a.m. Closing time Sunday to Thursday is 10:00 p.m., Friday and Saturday 11:00 p.m. There is no website yet, but they're working on it.

visiting her maternal grandmother's home on Smith Street. Why would she say such a thing now?

An apology and explanation came the next week during her concert at the Pontiac Silverdome: "I didn't mean the people of Bay City stink, just the Dow Chemical Plant." Yeah, right, easy to say to people who just spent three weeks' pay to get in to see her.

The rumor mill works overtime in Bay City with claims of "Madonna" sightings on the streets of downtown, occasionally passing by the home that still exists on Smith Street, or at the cemetery in Kawkawlin where her mother is buried. She was definitely spotted at her grandmother's funeral in March 2011 along with her four children. Elsie Fortin was 99 and buried at St. Mary of the Assumption Church. Word is Madonna ties a scarf around her head, wears dark sunglasses, and is still looking for that key.

(You may also glimpse Madonna at Ciccone Vineyards in Sutton's Bay, owned by her father, Tony.)

★ ★

Parrothead's Unite for Wildly Cheesy Fun
Caseville

Move over, Jimmy Buffett . . . Margaritaville has stormed into Michigan's thumb region for ten days of wackiness known as the "Cheeseburger in Paradise Festival."

From a three-foot-tall cheeseburger mailbox permanently stationed along State Highway 25 to pink flamingos, hula-skirt adorned pigs, and plastic palm trees, Caribbean whimsy saturates the town. Every business gets involved raising signs that say SERIOUS THOUGHTS PROHIBITED or TWO BLONDS AND A BUSINESS.

Check your inhibitions at the next town. Everyone here is ready to party hearty any time. After all, it's five o'clock somewhere. Margaritas flow through their veins with an occasional piña colada thrown in for variety, although no open alcoholic beverages are permitted on any streets.

Taking center stage is the cheeseburger, standard with cheddar or dressed up innovatively with bleu cheese, pineapple, or jalapeño pepper stuffed with sour cream. Vendors line the downtown area and every restaurant has added patio seating while their outdoor barbecue grills are smokin' hot.

There's something for everyone with a cheeseburger hairdo contest, cheeseburger eating contest, and Jimmy Buffett look-alikes. Dancing continues through the night to tunes by such groups as Parrots of the Caribbean.

No one will dispute the fact that the biggest attraction is the midweek extravaganza called the Parade of Tropical Fools, attracting more than 50,000 spectators who begin staking out their territory by setting up chairs at midnight the night before. And all the anticipation doesn't disappoint.

US Congresswoman Candice Miller was the grand marshal in 2011, marking possibly the only serious moment. The floats that followed were characteristically comedic: Tiki Bill's fully equipped bar complete with moving porta-potties, a majestic throne for the Caseville Bahama

Proving their passion for cheeseburgers, Hula "girls," pirates, and pink flamingos parade down Caseville's Main Street.

Mama, a young lady wrapped in a boa (not made of feathers, but rather a real live boa constrictor). An obstetrician cleverly promoted his business with a western theme and the words STIRRUPS AREN'T JUST FOR COWBOYS. A front loader atop another featured a reindeer that lifted his leg and shot water at the crowd. The Red Hat Ladies, likely in their 80s, rode by, all bearing large beaded necklaces from Hooters.

Simply stated, the whole parade is a hoot with some loot. Observers benefit by the tens of thousands of Mardi Gras beads thrown out. Or maybe you'll be lucky enough to catch a bag of Doritos, rolls of Smarties, or my personal favorite, gummy cheeseburgers.

Sponsored by the Caseville Chamber of Commerce, the festival's been expanding ever since it first began in 1999. Now spread over ten days, you can get the latest on this party by going to www.caseville chamber.net, or calling (989) 856-3818 or (800) 606-1347.

Walk Up and Touch the Stars

Move over, Grauman's Chinese Theatre. Step aside, Planet Hollywood. Make room for the Chesaning Showboat Star Walk.

Bobby Vinton, in 1991, was the first to bend over and place his hands in wet concrete, leaving his permanent impression for all to admire. Each year after that the Chesaning Showboat's headliners have been asked to repeat the process with their personal branding. There are now thirty-four Hollywood squares lining the pavement in front of the chamber of commerce office. They're not easy to spot from a distance and up close may even be mistaken for a set of gravestones, inscribed with the year of the star's appearance.

Don't let that scare you. Lots of people step forward to size up the palms. Anxious to see how I measured up to the big names, I tried my hand against Kenny Rogers . . . too big. Brenda Lee . . . too small. Frankie Valli . . . just right. Frankie Valli? I wanted to . . . but then I remembered, "Big Girls Don't Cry."

The Showboat Star Walk is right in front of the Chesaning Chamber of Commerce at 218 North Front Street. Call (800) 255-3055 or (989) 845-3055.

A fallen pebble turns out to be the perfect filler for Lesley Gore's thumbnail.

★ ★

Connector to the Mother-in-Law . . . Sweet

Croswell

Oozing with sugary sweetness from every corner—that's been the reputation of the city of Croswell for more than a century. The arrival of the Michigan Sugar Company inaugurated it all when it began lusciously converting more than three hundred tons of sugar beets into a reported 44,668,730 pounds of taste-satisfying crystals every year.

A bridge to mend troubled waters when the in-laws become out-laws.

At the turn of the twentieth century, all the hardworking townsfolk loved to enjoy their free time at River Bend Park on the west side of the Black River. It wasn't easy to reach, though: They were forced to hike a long, roundabout path available only from the south. In the summer of 1905 city officials raised $300 to build a footbridge across the river, spanning 139 feet.

Shortly after it was erected, David Wise, a major proponent of the project, put up an overhead sign on the west end declaring BE GOOD TO YOUR MOTHER-IN-LAW. No one's exactly sure why those words were chosen, although theories run rampant. Some say couples contemplating marriage would often walk hand-in-hand over the bridge. What better way to keep those hands together for eternity than with a little in-law coaching? Others say everyone knows to be nice to your mother, but a friendly reminder may be needed to ensure that kindness to a mother-in-law. Or possibly it's a retort to Ernest Wild's observation, "However much you dislike your mother-in-law you must not set fire to her."

Constructed of 455 wooden slats and standing twenty-five feet above water at its highest point, it shakes and creaks and rattles and rolls as you saunter across. Even the slightest external force (perhaps a nudge from an in-law?) may find you quickly engulfed in not-so-hot water.

Michigan's only suspension footbridge can be accessed by turning off Howard Avenue, the town's main thoroughfare, onto Maple. The renamed Swinging Bridge Park is right at the end. For more information call (819) 679-2299 or visit www.croswell-mich.com.

Puff Away: An Answer for Every Pipe Dream

Flint

Michigan is the only state in the Union that doesn't grow tobacco but does have a government proclamation for Pipe Smoker's Week. That's thanks to the efforts of Paul T. Spaniola, the world's foremost pipe authority and owner of Paul's Pipe Shop in downtown Flint since July 12, 1928. That's not a typo—Paul was just fifteen years old when he

★ ★

**Paul Spaniola has snuffed out the competition to earn
the designation of the world's greatest pipe smoker.**

opened his doors for business. His shelves now stock a million different smoking devices, one as artfully crafted as the next, running the
gamut from wooden cowboy boots and eighteen-carat gold umbrellas
to a $2.69 corncob pipe.

Always smoking, or "supposed to be," as founder of Paul's Institute
of Pipe Smoking, he taught Susan Hayward how to become a feminine
puffer for her role opposite Charlton Heston in the 1952 movie *The
President's Lady.*

Six-time world pipe-smoking champion (whoever can keep
3.3 grams of tobacco going the longest without relighting wins),

★ ★

Spaniola's personal collection, housed in the second-floor museum, includes the pipes of all the world champions since 1949. Also on display is his "trophy," the 1897 pipe of mega millionaire C. S. Mott, with whom he shared many a good smoke throughout Mott's seventy-five years of lighting up.

Spaniola holds dear the visitors from all over the world who stop in to say hi, catch one of his famous card tricks, or buy a pipe or two. As a sign of appreciation, for years he reciprocated by sending out birthday cards to every person who ever bought a pipe, a practice he abandoned after the post office changed its forwarding policy.

Born on January 29, 1913, this father of twelve (ten girls and two boys fighting for the bathroom), used to come into work every day to whip up one of his two hundred secret blends of tobacco, with fragrant whiffs of cherry vanilla, Georgia peach, chocolate, or Louisiana coffee grabbing you the minute you open the door.

Forget about all those highfalutin political theories. Hope for world harmony may lie in one tobacco-filled tube. As the gospel according to Paul Spaniola says, "If everybody smoked there would be no wars." Pass the peace pipe, please.

The Arrowhead Pipe Smoker's Club meets the third Tuesday of each month at Paul's Pipe Shop and Pipe Hospital (all brands of wounded pipes cheerfully healed) located at 647 South Saginaw Street. It's open Monday through Saturday. Spaniola is not there every day, but you're guaranteed to see at least one family member. You can reach the store at (810) 235-0581, check it out at www.iapsc.net/html/pauls .html (International Association of Pipe Smoker's Clubs), or find Paul's Pipe Shop on Facebook . . . yes, he has his own Facebook page.

Why Did the Chicken Cross the Road?*
Frankenmuth

*To get out of Frankenmuth.

Frankenmuth, Michigan, could be the model for towns that want to reinvent themselves.

★ ★

In the 1950s when the Interstate 75 expressway bypassed Highway 83, the city's main street, Frankenmuth had to react. The city fathers knew their town—which had become known to salesmen, hunters, fishermen, and tourists as a stop on their trip up north—needed an attraction. It was sister city Gunzenhausen, Germany, that realized the answer: the city's Germanic roots. They guessed right, and now Frankenmuth is one of the top tourist attractions in the state, drawing more than three million visitors annually.

According to the Frankenmuth Chamber of Commerce, the city's name comes from the Bavarian province of Franken; *muth* is German for "courage."

Courage was something the earliest missionaries had when they left their homes in Germany to come to the area to teach the Native Americans the ways of Christianity. Others from the same area followed, and before long the town was a Bavarian community, complete with the language and customs of their homeland. A big part of that heritage was the hospitality that necessitated hotels and restaurants in the city. Zehnder's of Frankenmuth is ranked the eighth largest restaurant in the nation based on total sales. Along with the Frankenmuth Bavarian Inn Restaurant, the town's landmark restaurants are known for "Frankenmuth-style" chicken dinners. Zehnder's alone serves approximately a million guests per year, who consume 900,000 pounds of chicken, 640 tons of cabbage, 130,000 pounds of vegetables, and produces 70,000 loaves of Stollen (fruit) bread. The third generation of Zehnders still serves family-style. The heaping platters of food would be enough to make even Elvis "Return to Zehnder's."

Still, as good as the food is, it takes more than a hearty meal to attract more than 2,000 motorcoach group tours annually. The city offers year-round activities beginning in winter with an international snow- and ice-carving contest. In May the World Expo of Beer takes over, with 150 types of brew from around the world available. In June the Bavarian Festival includes parades, arts and crafts shows, and (naturally) traditional German food.

Then on the Fourth of July you can try to get rid of all those calories in "Volkslaufe" or "People's Race," which draws more than 2,000 runners or roughly the same number found in line for a Sunday chicken dinner at Zehnder's.

The list of events never ends, but on the remote chance that the week you visit isn't part of a "something-fest," you can visit the woodcarvers, sausage makers, clock shops, winery, Glockenspiel Tower, and a partridge in a pear tree . . . down the road at Bronner's CHRISTmas Wonderland.

Frankenmuth is east off Interstate 75 between Flint and Saginaw. For information, call (800) FUN-TOWN—that's (800) 386-8696—or visit www.frankenmuth.org.

Bronner's CHRISTmas Wonderland
Frankenmuth

With all the talk about the commercialization of Christmas, you'd think the world's largest Christmas store would be front and center to begin holiday decorating just after the Fourth of July. But before you even get inside the seven and a quarter acres, or five and a half football fields, of Bronner's complex, that preconception disappears. For one thing, there's the spelling. Everywhere you look at Bronner's, the name of the store is written CHRISTmas Wonderland. That's not an accident. Nor is the Silent Night Memorial Chapel.

With special permission from the Oberndorf, Austria, city government, Bronner's erected a replica of that city's Silent Night Memorial Chapel. That original was built on the site of the St. Nicholas Church where "Silent Night" was first sung in 1818. The 56-foot-tall chapel was built in tribute to the famous Christmas hymn, and in thankfulness to God.

That same theme permeates everything. That's the way founder Wally Bronner wanted it when he started the business in 1945. Today, visitors can watch a twenty-minute video that gives the history, emphasizing the motto of the store: "Enjoy CHRISTmas, It's HIS Birthday; Enjoy Life, It's HIS Way."

At a height of seventeen feet, this bigger-than-life
Santa is one of three that's been greeting customers
at Bronner's for more than thirty years.

WAYNE BRONNER

★ ★

Better than two million visitors pass through the doors every year. In fact, during the single weekend after Thanksgiving, over 50,000 shoppers check out everything from Nativity scenes to mistletoe with 6,000-plus styles of decorations, including Merry Christmas greeting ornaments in more than seventy languages. There are so many lights around the store, every inch is lit up, well, like a Christmas tree. The monthly electric bill averages $900 a day.

Bronner's has more than seventy billboards around the country, including the one on Interstate 75 near Ocala, Florida, just north of Disney World.

Bronner's CHRISTmas Wonderland is found at 25 Christmas Lane. Call (989) 652-9931 or, for recorded information, (800) ALL-YEAR (255-9327). Visit them on the web at www.bronners.com. Bronner's is open 361 days a year.

Fixin' Your Bird
Frankenmuth

Ever wonder where to go if your cuckoo won't "cooke"?

The Frankenmuth Clock Company has heard it all. Head cuckoo corrector Carol Wilcox says that since the clocks are mechanical, the biggest problems are caused by a lack of maintenance. The clocks should be cleaned and oiled every few years. And indeed, customers come here from all over the Midwest to get their birds oiled by Wilcox and company and see the more than 1,000 clocks in the store.

Cuckoo clock aficionados will tell you that there are two types of birds: musical and nonmusical. You also have a choice of a one-day clock or the seven-day variety, both of which are wound by pulling up a traditionally pinecone-shaped weight on a chain that gradually travels down and moves the inner workings of the clock. That chain is probably why the cuckoo wristwatch was never a big seller.

Cuckoo clocks date back to 1760 in the Black Forest of Germany. One of the local clockmakers got tired of the same old chime sound that was commonly used and replaced the bell tone with the cuckoo bird native to the area. The body of the cuckoo clock we know today is made to resemble a railway stationhouse, which evolved after the railroad came to the Black Forest.

The original clocks were made completely of wood, and many of today's clocks are still hand-carved. They range in size from small wall versions to a grandfather cuckoo clock made by the Dold Company in Germany. The 6½-foot clock is hand-carved out of basswood and includes a seventy-three-note Swiss music box that plays two different tunes. The carvings include two horses, a water fountain, a little boy, and a little Bavarian forest. If Bill Gates were a cuckoo, this clock is where he would live.

The choices of clocks vary from the simple single-bird model to versions that include dancers coming out of various doors of the railroad station spinning to a variety of musical tunes.

Imagine the Radio City Music Hall Rockettes and the Village People in lederhosen. In fact, I think one of the Village People did wear lederhosen.

Don't be disappointed if the hour passes and all the cuckoo clocks in the shop don't sound off. The birds are all safe in their houses until someone asks for a demonstration.

I personally would like a cuckoo that sounded like a flute, but even the Frankenmuth Clock Company doesn't have one flute over the cuckoo's nest. The store is located at 966 South Main; (989) 652-2933. Open seven days a week, 9:00 a.m. to 6:30 p.m. For more information visit www.frankenmuthclock.com.

Eight Sides Are Better than Four
Gagetown

It's Michigan's largest eight-sided barn and it sits practically in the middle of nowhere. Driving up to it, you'd think you were in Kansas, where the roads are flat surrounded by farmland.

That's the case in Gagetown, where the thumb's Octagon Barn garners attention from admirers across the country. Part of the 520-acre

Mud Lake Estate, it was constructed in 1923 by the president of the Gagetown State Savings Bank, James Purdy.

It's unlike any barn built at that time in Michigan. First, it's tall, standing about four stories high at seventy feet. The octagon is formed by eight outside walls, each 42½ feet high, creating 8,600 square feet of space. A twenty-nine-foot loft provides another 6,200 square feet of elevated storage space. In short, there's plenty of room for any animal . . . Noah's entire ark would have fit without a problem.

When you step inside, you feel as if you're in the middle of an old western movie. You hear creaks and squeaks from the constant breeze that filters throughout, and it's easy to envision farmers pitching mega barrels of hay. The barn is filled with farming memorabilia, like the 1908 New Deere Cylinder Hayloader.

Officially the Octagon Barn is open only for special activities. Tours usually occur in August, followed by Fall Family Days in September. Typically it's then locked up at the end of October.

While the gate outside the property is locked, the barn itself most often is not. So you're free to walk about at your leisure. The Friends of the Thumb Octagon just ask that you sign the guest book and turn the lights out when you leave. Contact them at PO Box 145, Gagetown, Michigan 48735; (989) 665-0081; www.thumboctagonbarn.org.

The barn can be found, though not easily, 1½ miles east of Gagetown at 6948 Richie Road, north of Bay City Forestville Road in Tuscola County. Signs point the way.

Lawn Ornament Capital of the World

Lennon

Somewhere, someone is losing sleep right now worried over how he's ever going to find the ideal adornment to spice up his boring lawn. Rest assured, Michigan has the concrete solution.

Acres of cement figurines shaped like gargoyles, sombreros, turtles, and anything else that's ever appeared in your worst nightmare fill the outside of Krupp's Novelty Shop.

✦ ✦

It's the brainchild of Jean Krupp, who in 1950 was so poor she started selling wooden doghouses made out of trashed orange crates on her front lawn. Acting on a suggestion to include the sale of concrete birdbaths, her assortment expanded and so did her profits.

More than half a century later, on the same front yard where it all started, rows and rows of indescribable "stuff" are organized with a hint of madness to their method. Signage over Row 5B introduces angels, fire hydrants, and fruit baskets. Farther down, it's an aisle of jockeys and Dutch couples.

Customer buying habits change. For a while their biggest sellers were "bend-over butts," but that trend has fallen through the cracks. Now it's anything that spews water, except maybe their re-creation of Michelangelo's *David*, which was found by a shopper to be anatomically incorrect in its proportions.

Inside, the store hosts collectibles and things not so collectible . . . like that decoupaged plaque of Elvis.

Is there anything too tacky to sell? Employees say they've almost given up on finding a good home for the toilet bowl planter. I'll bet somewhere, someone is tossing and turning that around in his or her dreams at this very moment.

Krupp's Home and Garden Décor crowds the corner of Highways 21 and 13, aka 2011 Sheridan Avenue. It's open seven days a week; call (810) 621-3752.

Wimps Only, Please
Lexington

The sign over the register reads, PRICES SUBJECT TO CHANGE ACCORDING TO CUSTOMER'S ATTITUDE. Wimpy's Place is all about attitude. The food almost seems secondary to the fun that exudes from the staff.

You may find the crew annoying when they badger you to order more or call out to other diners that it's your fault orders are delayed because you're taking so long to make up your mind.

★ ★

The menu is small, but then so is the interior, with room for only
forty-nine customers, and that includes the dozen counter seats.
Founded in 1987 by Jim and Cindy Gresock (just remember greasy sock),
its mainstay is the burgers. The more you eat, the greater your chances
of making it into the Belly Bomber Hall of Fame. All it takes is the consumption of twelve of Wimpy's burgers in an hour or less. Think it can't
be done? Think again . . . at last count there were thirty-two members,

Ceiling to Floor . . . Confections and More

Right next
door to
Wimpy's (at
7272 Huron

Avenue in Lexington) is the 150-year-old Lexington General Store,
where I picked up my new favorite wall hanging reminding me, GOOD
FRIENDS ARE LIKE FAT THIGHS, THEY ALWAYS KEEP IN TOUCH.

Your search for all those impossible-to-find candies of yesteryear
will end right here. Baskets are on overload with Sen-Sen and bags
of old-fashioned hard candy including horehound and sassafras,
while your sweet tooth's memory will be tempted by oodles of penny
candy, now inflationarily priced at two cents.

The Lexington General Store is open Monday through Sunday. Call
(810) 359-8900.

with one good eater setting the record at nineteen. Appointments are necessary for this ultimate consumption test.

Cases filled with Wimpy memorabilia line the walls. What doesn't fit in the case winds up in the Gresocks' basement. Word is that their home is crammed with every Wimpy product ever made, including a Popeye PacMan machine.

A general store where candy counters outnumber all other goods.

There's added incentive to chow down here—25% SENIOR CITIZEN DISCOUNT . . . OFFERED AT 100 YEARS OF AGE, ACCOMPANIED BY BOTH PARENTS AND MUST SHOW PHOTO ID.

Wimpy's Place opens every day for breakfast at 7:00 a.m.; closing time varies according to the season. It can be found at 7270 Huron Avenue in the heart of downtown Lexington. Call (810) 359-5450 or check it out online at www.wimpysplace.com.

Here Comes Santa and Santa and Santa and Santa and . . .
Midland

To be Santa is a privilege, not a job. That's the motto of the Charles W. Howard Santa School, the oldest Santa school in the world. It originated in 1937 in Albion, New York, but has been housed in Midland, Michigan, since 1987, when Tom Valent became the school's third dean in history.

Valent says he "had a calling" to be Santa and wants to share his enthusiasm for the jolly man in the red suit with the rest of the world. He doesn't advertise and even shies away from publicity for fear it may spoil some of the magic for children.

Yet each October, people from all over the world convene in Midland's Santa House to hone their skills at playing St. Nick. Besides Santa from Disney World and every mall imaginable, there have been Santas from Sweden, Switzerland, Australia, and England. The school has even done a tour of duty in Greenland, being named the official host of the first World Santa Claus Summit.

So what do people learn in Santa School? While the textbook and basic principles remain the same as they were sixty-five years ago, there has been updating. In addition to the heart and spirit of Santa, students today learn how to sing, use sign language, and give TV and radio interviews.

And cosmetics is another issue . . . the cost of playing Santa isn't cheap. Equipment can run up to $4,000 with custom-made hair and beard.

A school where there are absolutely no exceptions to the dress code and clean-shaven faces are strictly forbidden.
HOLLY VALENT, SANTA CLAUS SCHOOL

Tom's wife, Holly, has made sure that classes are all now politically correct, with about 25 percent female attendees learning how to portray Mrs. Santa Claus.

Santa School operates as a nonprofit organization. The cost is $400 for three days . . . $350 if you're a returning student . . . a real bargain for the opportunity to bring a lifetime of happiness to children.

Classes are held in the Santa House, which is open to the public free of charge from December 1 to December 28. The personification of Christmas, it's a veritable delight for the senses and offers the opportunity to see the collection of six-foot-tall nutcrackers and other magnificent woodwork that Valent has masterfully handcrafted.

The Valents are one amazing couple, who live and breathe Christmas 365 days a year. With five children of their own, they've added two reindeer to their household, Comet and Cupid, both females. In fact, I'll share a secret. All of Santa's reindeer are female because the males lose their antlers before winter. And what would the sleigh look like without antlers on the reindeer? It's true, Rudolph is really a girl.

The Santa House is located in downtown Midland on the corner of Main and Highway 20 (Isabella Road). For more information call (989) 631-0587 or log on to www.santaclausschool.com.

Smile, Say Pinconning
Pinconning

Pinconning is an Indian word meaning "place of potatoes." Then why is it designated as "Michigan's cheese capital" when no place in town makes cheese? Now, *cheese potato capital* I could understand.

To set the record straight, in 1915 local boy Dan Horn was doing a little cross-breeding of cheese recipes when he fell upon a mix that won the taste buds of both young and old. Patent-protecting his golden wedges from imitators, he assigned them the name of their birthplace: Pinconning.

Nowadays the formula remains the same, a cross between colby and cheddar, but the last plant here closed in 1995 so all the cheese wizardry is performed at an undisclosed location in the UP then hauled back to Horn's hometown for distribution to wholesale and retail markets.

The oldest of the brood is Wilson's Cheese Shoppe, founded in 1939 by Horn's daughter, who let the patent expire. Each year 125 tons of the partially homespun product goes out its doors; the aging process still takes up space in local coolers. With cheese, the older it gets, the more people like it. Like a memorable kiss, the measurement of perfection comes if it "melts in your mouth and bites your tongue at the same time."

Since 1965 this giant mouse has been standing guard,
never once leaving his post over the cheese at Wilson's.

Thanks to Wilson's, the rest of the country knows what the word *Pinconning* really stands for. Located at 130 North Highway 13, Wilson's Cheese Shoppe is open 364 days a year, closed on Christmas. Call (989) 879-2002 or (800) 243-3735 (800-CHEESE5) or go to www .wilsoncheese.com.

★ ★

Brother, Can You Spare a Dime?

Port Huron

Calling all international travelers! Here's your opportunity to experience two countries at one time, no matter what your budget. Just hop
on the Blue Water Trolley. For one full hour, you'll be given a first-class
introduction to forty-six of the top attractions in Port Huron, including a panoramic view of the Blue Water Bridge that leads to Canada.
You'll be up-close and personal with freighters from all over the world
as they pass through the St. Clair River on their way to Lake Huron.
Filling you in on historical details and anecdotal stories of the city is a
real live tour guide . . . no prerecorded narratives here. The fare for the
journey? Just one thin dime. (Anyone over 60, handicapped, or with a
valid Medicare card pays only a nickel.)

That's been the price since 1986 when the trolley was first acquired
by the Blue Water Area Transit, and there are no plans to raise it.
Between early June and mid-October, about 2,200 travelers take
advantage of the best bargain in town, possibly the world. You can do
the math. There's not a lot of revenue there. Consequently, you may
have to look at a few ads from places like Port Huron Paint or Bowl-A-
Drome/Zebra Bar. But no one seems to mind when you can save some
hard-earned dollars. There are reasons the rich are getting richer. Even
Texas billionaire Ross Perot jumped on for the ten-cent jaunt when he
was in town.

During the summer it runs Monday through Saturday, 10:00 a.m. to
4:00 p.m. (Sunday until 2:00 p.m.). For more information and possible
schedule changes, contact Blue Water Area Transit at (810) 987-7373
or visit www.bwbus.com/bluewatertrolley.htm.

Thomas Alva Edison: An Educator's Nightmare

Port Huron

Thomas Edison is quite likely the only person on earth to have been
rejected by a school district, and years later have that same system
name a school for him.

Thomas Edison got his big break at this train depot, now dwarfed by the massive Blue Water Bridge.

In 1854 Edison's family moved to Port Huron, when Edison was just seven. A bout with scarlet fever left him with a serious, yet misunderstood, hearing loss, prompting his teachers to find him dull, officially labeling him "addled." Infuriated, his mother tried two other schools, with no success, and subsequently concluded that homeschooling would be the best answer.

On October 10, 1965, the Port Huron Schools apparently had a change of heart, dedicating their newest school Thomas A. Edison Elementary.

In the early 1860s, Edison sold newspapers and snacks on the Grand Trunk Railroad, escaping boredom by building a printing press and mobile chemistry lab, igniting a fire on board during one of his phosphorus experiments.

All has been forgiven and, in 2001, the Thomas Edison Depot Museum opened, allowing visitors a hands-on opportunity to create the world's next technological novelty in the same spot where the lightbulb first went off inside young Tom's mind.

The Depot Museum sits dwarfed under the Blue Water Bridge, north of Thomas Edison Parkway. (Isn't it funny how many things here are now named for this classroom failure?) Admission is charged. Call (810) 982-0891 or visit www.phmuseum.org.

Teahouse of the Saginaw Moon
Saginaw

Enter quietly and at your own risk of embarrassment as you comply with the ban on shoes. If ever you needed an excuse for a pedicure or a good reason to darn that hole in your sock, this is it: the traditional tea ceremony at the Japanese teahouse in downtown Saginaw.

Bred from a partnership with Saginaw's sister city, Tokushima, Japan, the teahouse is as authentic as it gets here in the States, incorporating classic Japanese architecture in its tongue-and-groove construction, without the use of one solitary nail. Unique in their sisterhood, both cities shared in the 1986 building costs and hold joint ownership of the land.

In Japan devotees spend a lifetime studying Teaism. In Saginaw you can spend an hour in an escape halfway around the world through the ceremonial high tea (Chado).

Only the best—the professed-healthy green tea powder, not the Bigelow bags we think are so rare, along with some sort of sweet—is delivered via a kimono-clad server.

When you're finished, a stroll through the tree-filled gardens will walk off the eighty-two calories consumed.

★ ★

Daily tours of the teahouse at 527 Ezra Rust Drive and Washington are open to walk-ins. The ceremonial tea, held the second Saturday of each month, requires a reservation. Private ceremonies are available with a minimum of ten people. Charges range from $3 to $8. Call (989) 759-1648 for more information, or check out www.japanese culturalcenter.org.

Phony Baloney Here . . . Real Thing Takes Center Stage
Yale

The sign outside the First Presbyterian Church downtown sets the scene: GOD IS GOOD AND SO IS YALE BOLOGNA. There's no question that everyone in town is wild over this bologna. In 1989 they designated the last weekend in July as the Bologna Festival and they've been celebrating that weekend ever since. That's when the relatively small town with 2,000 residents swells to over 20,000 fanatical fans.

Under the big top is the main attraction: locally made bologna. You can have it fried in a sandwich (tastes a bit like a flattened hot dog), on a stick, or a two-pound ring, regular or jalapeño and cheese.

Lots of "meaty" activities fill the days: the crowning of the Bologna King and Queen, the crowning of the Bologna Babies, the goofy golf cart contest, and the Saturday evening Bologna Parade.

If your mouth is watering to find out how this tasty treat is made, Roy's meat processing opens its doors for tours and more information than your salivary glands may be able to handle. Yale started making the bologna in 1924, and the Roy family has been involved since 1936. You'll first step into the retail outlet, where you can purchase numerous choices of flavored bologna: mac and cheese, pepper, olive, onion, and even pizza. After that, it's into the slaughter room, with a slightly eerie executioner feel (and smell) to it, followed by a walk into the frozen meat locker. Despite being surrounded by dozens of hanging cows, lamb, and bull (bologna is 62 percent bull, the rest pork and secret seasonings), the experience was refreshing at thirty-four degrees, a nice change from the blistering heat outside.

The Pink Boa-Lognas and Pirates of Baloneyville parade
by King Bologna.

To relieve the steaminess of the day, back in town, the Yale Fire
Department shoots out water to hose down the receptive crowd
while the Yale Keystone Cops park their Squirt Gun Express for more
drenching fun.

The whole weekend lives up to the town's claim, "Full of baloney,
and proud of it."

The Bologna Festival is sponsored by the Yale Chamber of Commerce. For more information you can visit them at 212 S. Main Street
(inside of Regional Realty), call them at (810) 387-YALE (9253), or visit
their website at www.yalechamber.com.

★ ★

C. Roy Meat Processing is located at 444 Roy Drive and is open Monday through Friday; (810) 387-3957. They give tours throughout the year upon request. On festival Saturday, "limo" golf carts will chauffeur you there from downtown (and that's no bull-oney).

You Say Tomato . . .

If you live in Michigan, do you call yourself a Michiganian or a Michigander? Your final answer may depend on how long you've been a resident. Lifers are the ganders, settlers are ganians. At least that's one theory.

Abraham Lincoln is blamed for starting the controversy with a pre-presidential visit here in 1848 when he sarcastically referred to a political rival as a "Michigander."

We're the only state that can't seem to make up its mind. Lawmakers have tried forever to reach a compromise on our true identity, but so far, thanks to their indecision, we shall officially remain nameless.

Even the state's two largest newspapers can't agree . . .

The *Detroit News* takes the position we're Michiganians.

The *Detroit Free Press* calls us all Michiganders.

If that's the case, maybe women should be called Michigeese.

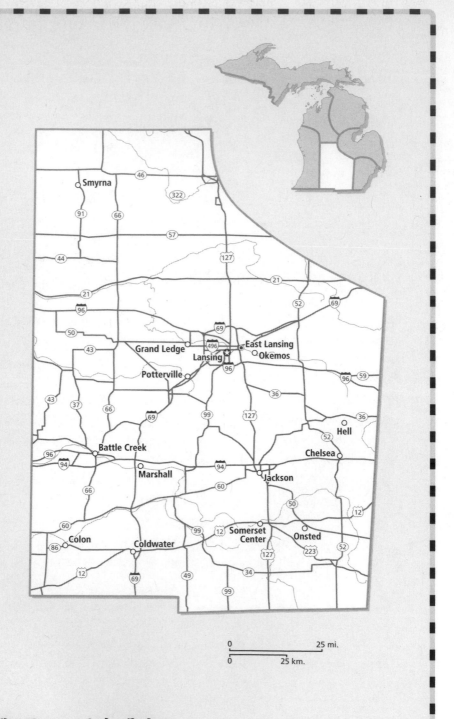

The Heart of the Palm

3

The Heart of the Palm

This is the *pulse point of Michigan, where the main arteries filter through the diverse landscape, extending a rhythmic lifeline to the more than nine million people in its grasp.*

Lansing, the state's capital, was situated as close to a geographic center as possible at the time of its appointment, when arguments arose that it was not close enough to the Great Lakes. Perhaps no one realized then that no matter where you stand in Michigan, you're never more than eighty-five miles away from one of those five major bodies of water. Nowadays it's a toss-up whether we're better represented by Lansing's lugnut-topped chimney or the nineteen Tiffany of New York–designed chandeliers in the Capitol Building. (I vote for the chimney; it's easier to clean.)

A town originally named Milton witnessed a skirmish between a surveyor and a band of Potawatomis by the side of a rather obscure river. The surveyor must have been victorious since he changed the name of both the river and the town to Battle Creek, where one Saturday in June you can have a grrrreat day chasing Tony the Tiger around at the world's longest breakfast table, a tradition commemorating the days when the city was home to more than one hundred cereal makers.

Either magic wands or pitchforks will get you in this neck of the woods. The town of Colon pulls in thousands for the country's largest magic convention even though there's not a single hotel room within miles of the city limits. And if that doesn't satisfy you, well, then you can go to Hell and back for a devil of a good time. It's just about an hour away.

And I'd be remiss in not mentioning the "heart" is the home of Michigan State University with its terra-cotta statue of Sparty (which underwent a bronze transformation, possibly to deter the blue spray paint he's subjected to during the annual MSU–U of M football game) and prizewinning chocolate cheese, which honestly tastes much better than it sounds.

The curious heart of Michigan, housing Houdini, a tuba museum, and the Republican Party.

★ ★

Even Without a Microwave It's Ready in a Jiffy
Chelsea

Ask anyone in the charmingly quaint town of Chelsea about their famous signature blue boxes and they won't be talking about Tiffany. Instead they'll tell you about their own clever packaging filled with the quick-baking Jiffy Mix.

Mabel White Holmes, whose husband, Howard, owned the Chelsea Milling Company, is the mastermind behind the product. In 1930, predating both Martha Stewart and Rachael Ray, she noticed one of her son's friends eating a biscuit resembling a merger of a hockey puck and a gum eraser. Determined to change that, she began blending ingredients to come up with a solution "so simple even a man can do it." Her concoction brought back memories of a family cook, who ordered her to "Tell your father them good, hot biscuits will be ready in a jiffy." Hence, the home baking mix market was born.

Today, business at Jiffy Mix is booming with twenty-two different varieties sold in every state plus China, Japan, and New Zealand. Yet 100 percent of the product remains Michigan-made. All the grains are grown here, and even those cute little boxes that boast "made in Michigan" are constructed of recycled cardboard and printed with soy-based ink.

You're invited to experience the manufacturing process first-hand during one of their factory tours, where excitement and enthusiasm oozes out of every inch of the facility. A friendly guide escorts you to the theater for an entertaining and informative movie starring the company's president and CEO, Howdy (Howard) Holmes, Mabel's grandson. Occasionally the former Indy race car driver will walk in afterward for some lively banter and Q & A. In addition to running the company, he's a natural showman with a quick (or jiffy-filled) wit.

The factory is impressive, churning out 1.6 million boxed products a day with lightning speed and precision. Each of the seventeen assembly lines can be adjusted to kick out anywhere between forty-five and seventy-five boxes a minute.

Jiffy Mix "towers" over Chelsea, keeping a
watchful eye over downtown.

At the end, you'll get a blue bag filled with a recipe book and a couple of boxes of muffin mix (corn is their number one seller; we got blueberry).

Unlike their competitors who spend millions on marketing costs, Jiffy spends nothing, relying instead on word of mouth to get out their message of high quality with great value. Some 19,000 people who take the tour annually are likely telling their friends, "Ain't muffin but the real thing here."

The hour-long tours with refreshments are offered three times a day, Monday through Friday, for ages six and up. Reservations are required. Call (800) 727-2460 or (734) 475-1361. Jiffy mixes at 201 W. North Street in downtown Chelsea. Their website is www.jiffymix .com.

★ ★

Lean on Me

Chelsea

Seitz's Tavern is home to Michigan's longest-standing stand-up bar. Sound like double talk? Not at all. Oh sure, at twenty-three feet it's long, but it's unmatched anywhere because it never had and never will have any seats. At least not as long as it stays in the Seitz family, where it's been since 1916.

A jovial fellow with a welcoming smile, third-generation owner Randy Seitz is determined to maintain the tradition of resting only your feet and not your bottom. Besides being more conducive to conversation, the decision makes good business sense. Instead of accommodating only a dozen or so stools, throngs can get up-close and personal at the counter.

Any Saturday in June, entire wedding parties can be spotted making their descent for the $4.25 beef plate: three pieces of bread, beef, onions, and all the merriment a newlywed cocktail hour can provide.

Rubbing elbows with the unexpected is part of the charm—whether it's one of the regulars or a real live party animal, like the horse that stopped in for some waterin' down during the Centennial Celebration. Over the years hunters have been known to drop in with their conquests, some leaving long-lasting impressions such as the fella who burst in hurling his trophy bag of bull . . . frogs, leaving them to croak about, literally, for days.

Situated in the shadows of the silos of the Jiffy Food Mixes—you know, those popular baking mixes that have become staples in American households—third-generation customers now bring in their own children of all ages to experience this old-time legacy.

You'll find Seitz's Tavern at 110 West Middle Street in downtown Chelsea. Call (734) 475-7475. Open Monday through Saturday 7:00 a.m. until 1:00 or 2:00 a.m. Grandma Seitz's rule prevails today: closed on Sunday, allowing her to go to church and Grandpa to go fishin'. Cash only. (Seitz's is up for sale, so call ahead for any possible changes.)

★ ★

Thousands "Bear" All for a Friendly Hug
Chelsea

Imagine being greeted by a seven-foot-tall grizzly bear—with a smile on its face. That's exactly what you encounter as you step inside the Teddy Bear Factory and Toy Museum.

A quick glance around the retail outlet and you'll see thousands of teddy bears, some with zippers up their backs, waiting for a tender touch of stuffing. After acquiring an adoption certificate, a bear bathtub is available for use, complete with a floating rubber ducky.

Owning a teddy bear is much like owning a doll, which means it needs a wardrobe. Racks of sailor suits, cowgirl apparel, Halloween costumes, and imprintable hoodies make sure that your bear doesn't have to go home bear-naked.

Through the large picture window, you'll see what they claim is the world's largest "real" teddy bear. No one there was quite sure what that meant. They just knew he was big, likely over 1,000 pounds, with one arm alone weighing a hefty fifty pounds.

Also in open view are rows and rows of boxes filling the 35,000-square-foot warehouse, each "bearing" the words "Made in China" (or Indonesia). That was disappointing, yet the museum guarantees that each and every bear is "designed" right here in Michigan.

At a nearby table, women are putting finishing touches on custom animals. In this case they were stitching up the stinger on Georgia Tech's mascot, Buzz the Bee, to be shipped to the university. Surprisingly, the Teddy Bear Museum says their number-one customer is the US Navy, sending bears to their military bases around the world. Guess that explains the need for sailor suits.

Back in the showroom, lining the side wall is the Toy Museum, taking you through a visual history of playthings. A 1905 sixteen-inch Steiff Bear is featured, along with goodies like a Schuco yes/no bear from the 1920s, a 1918 Bing sewing machine, and a 1940s swinging Pinocchio ring toss.

Three hundred sixty teddy bears fill up 46.5 square feet of this record-setting flag.

Be sure to look up high so you don't miss the world's largest teddy bear flag, a *Guinness* World Record holder.

Factory tours are available every non-holiday Saturday at 11:00 a.m., 1:00 p.m., and 3:00 p.m. School and group tours are available weekdays by appointment. Open Monday through Saturday 10:00 a.m. to 6:00 p.m. and Sunday noon to 5:00 p.m. at 400 Main Street. For information call (734) 433-5499 or visit www.chelseateddybear.com.

Reel-Time Retro
Coldwater

While many people think of the drive-in movie as a mecca for making out, my mother insisted she went there with someone she really didn't like, so no one else would see her with an embarrassing date. Whatever the reason, for nearly forty years people have continued to flock to the Capri Drive-in in Coldwater.

Founded in 1964 by John and Mary Magocs, today it remains somewhat of a big-screen version of *All in the Family.* On any given night you'll see current owners Tom and Sue Magocs and their three children among the crew bagging popcorn or cleaning the restrooms. Their brood's total dedication to the movie biz is the reason they believe they're one of only eight drive-ins still in operation in Michigan.

It's always family-focused at the Capri, with close to 1,000 cars and trucks (the tallest to the back, please), packed with parents, kids, and pets. Before showtime Frisbees are flying through the air and out come the lawn chairs for a best-seat-in-the-house view of the star-filled sky. When the sun goes down, the "reel" magic begins, transforming acres of dirt into a Hollywood happening.

Named one of America's top ten drive-in theaters in both the *New York Times* and *USA Today,* an evening here is a blast from the past, with two first-run double features projected on futuristic-sized 115-by-75 foot screens. Even IMAX screens can't claim measurements of those proportions. What's really nifty about the whole setup is that everyone in your party doesn't have to watch the same movie. With the proper positioning you can enjoy the sight and state-of-the art stereo sound of one movie transmitted through your vehicle's radio, while someone else faces the opposite direction and receives the soundtrack of the alternative feature via portable radio. Talk about going to extremes to keep peace in the family.

The season begins weekends-only in March, and has been known to get a snowy kickoff with windshield wipers going into overtime, and commences into full swing, seven days a week, May through October. Curtain time is at dusk, usually fifteen to twenty minutes after sunset, with the box office opening two hours prior—7:00 p.m. in spring, 8:00 p.m. In summer. A cafeteria-style snack bar stands ready to fill the needs of the fans with hot dogs, hamburgers, and cans of bug spray. Which reminds me . . . maybe they should start selling Windex since the night I viewed the latest *Spider-Man* flick he appeared to be splattered with a few too many lifelike creatures.

The Capri Drive-in Theater sits at 119 West Chicago Road. Call (517) 278-5628 or visit their website at www.capridrive-in.com. Admission is charged.

All Horsepower Curbed Here

You can do almost everything in Coldwater without leaving the comfort of your car.

With a flick of your turn signal, someone will hop to your service at Allen's Root Beer Drive-In. The menu is mostly reflective of its 1950 beginnings, though some updating has occurred—bubble gum and margarita are now among the eighteen varieties of slushes.

Kids are especially fond of the ice cream cones capped with a sugar-coated eyeball. If your pooch is spotted through the window, he'll be treated to a free doggy sundae complete with chewy bone topping.

Allen's Root Beer Drive-In dishes up delights at 378 West Chicago. Hours vary with the season. Call (517) 279-9048.

★ ★

If the Headstone Is Whitestone, It's Blackstone

Colon

Hollywood doesn't stand alone in issuing maps for celebrity grave sightings. The Colon Community Historical Society has put out a detailed schematic of nineteen of some of the world's finest magicians who have chosen to have Lakeside Cemetery as the scene of their "final act."

Viewings can take place without ever leaving the comfort of your car. Most markers are tall enough to spot while taking a leisurely drive through the seven straight-and-narrow pathways that will take you alongside such conjurors as Donald (Monk) Watson, who in vaudeville was teamed with Benjamin Kubelsky, later known as Jack Benny.

Fans of the 1950s show *Milky the Clown* will recognize the name Karrell Fox, whose epitaph fittingly reads IT WAS FUN.

Of course the most frequently visited grave site is that of Harry Blackstone, marked with a contemporary carved white stone. Three generations are buried here: Harry Sr., the first "Blackstone the Great"; Harry Jr., who became a magician only after producing Broadway's *Hair* and TV's *The Smothers Brothers Comedy Hour;* and Harry III, crushed by a broken car hoist while changing oil following his 1984 return home from the US Marines.

Some of Blackstone's admirers are moved to tears, while others are moved to their wallets for coins, which are often seen lying at the base of the monument.

The last curtain call goes to "Little Johnny Jones," who left these words immortalized on his tombstone: NOW I HAVE TO GO AND FOOL ST. PETER.

Colon Lakeside Cemetery is located one mile west of the blinking light while you're looking east toward the village of Colon. You can pick up one of the maps at Abbott's Magic Company, 124 St. Joseph Street; (616) 432-3235.

Unexplainable images, invisible to the naked eye, have shown up on photos of this "spirit-filled" tombstone, marking the graves of three Harry Blackstones.
TRAVEL MICHIGAN

★ ★

Big Smiles. Say Cheese . . . Chocolate Cheese
East Lansing

For years Michigan State University has had one of the most highly regarded Food Science and Human Nutrition programs in the country. Leave it to "Moo U" to develop a confectionary concoction that would both melt the hearts of chocolate lovers everywhere and serve as a possible preventative for osteoporosis.

Is it dairy? Is it candy? Neither, exclusively. It's chocolate cheese. And it's been satisfying the cravings of Spartans since 1968, when Professor Dr. T. Hedrick and dairy plant manager A. V. Armitage put their curds together and invented an appetizing use for cheese scraps.

The ingredients read: 41 percent cheese, 29 percent powdered sugar, 13 percent nonfat dry milk, 12 percent butter, and 5 percent cocoa. Then they added some peanuts for definition and came up with chocolate cheese, or, as some might call it, cheesy fudge.

A possible oxymoron, the recipe has been a blue-ribbon winner at the Michigan State Fair every year it's entered. In fact, you can forget about the Rose Bowl or the Final Four. The truly big cheese title goes to chocolate cheese when, in 2000, it won the designation of "Grand Champion Cheese."

The MSU Dairy Store has been carrying the chocolate cheese for nearly forty years and sells nearly 1,000 pounds annually. Not bad, considering that's the only place in the world the secret formula cheese is available. In 2006 the dairy store began marketing on the Internet, so expect those figures to surpass the stratosphere any day now.

A hot spot with students and visitors, the Dairy Store, originally open for only two hours on Fridays, is now open seven days a week, dishing out thirty-seven flavors of ice cream. Crowd pleasers are spiced pumpkin in the fall and year-round Sesquicentennial Swirl developed for the University's 150th anniversary in 2005. Starting with a base of birthday cake batter ice cream, and swirled with green and white cake pieces and thick green icing variegated throughout, the flavor is one operations manager John Engstrom says he "wouldn't dare cancel." Apparently anything green sells well on campus. Except maybe cheese.

Self-guided tours of the dairy plant are available every day. If they're not manufacturing at the time you're there, an excellent twenty-eight-minute multimedia presentation will fill you in. Then you can fill up your tummy at the store in the same building. The MSU Dairy is located at 1140 South Anthony Hall, Farm Lane, East Lansing, or you can place your order for chocolate cheese, cheddar, dagano, or colby jack at www.shop.msu.edu or by calling (517) 355-8466.

A Heart-Worming Cliffhanger
Grand Ledge

Three hundred million years ago, Grand Ledge was a sea of salt water. Today what's left are layers of sandstone (the grand ledges) lining the banks of the Grand River, forming the biggest and best (and only) public rock climbing venue in the state.

History surrounds the site, although some of it is only accessible by ascending the forty-foot cliffs. (City officials say they're sixty feet; climbers tell a different story.) Some 12,000 people each year don their sporting gear and make the ascent in search of carvings, murals, and the rare flowering harebell plant, found only on bluffs and dunes.

An equally hearty number choose to keep their feet on the ground as spectators, either following the wooden-staired path or looking down on the action, watching as quietly as in a fishing tournament to see what's hooked at the end of the rope.

There's no question, cliffhangers are a rare breed with a softer side than their daredevil actions may lead you to believe. Take the group of climbers who one day, in a nesting area for cliff swallows, found a family of starving, motherless babies. Immediately they ceased their climb, digging up worms to hand-feed the little ones, repeating their nurturing routine each day for weeks until they were able to watch their "adoptees" fly away on their own to live happily ever after.

For the safest way to protect both yourself and the environment, it's best to get formal instruction. Vertical Ventures has been educating climbers in Grand Ledge's Oak Park for more than twenty years. Call them at (517) 420-4341 or click on their website: www.vertical-ventures.net. Oak Park, with its sandstone cliffs, can be reached off Front Street downtown. For more information check out www.grand ledge climbing.com.

The Road to Hell Is Paved With . . .

Hell

"Excuse me, could you please tell me how I go to Hell?" The clerk manages a chuckle. He hears it all the time. Fifteen minutes later I've arrived . . . in Hell, a three-store, 166-person town.

The only "Hell" anywhere on earth, its christening is credited to George Reeves, who in 1841 when asked for his opinion of the no-name enclave, brusquely replied, "You can name it Hell for all I care."

Today's demonic mastermind is John Colone, who gave up his day job as owner of a Chrysler dealership to become Odem Plenty, mayor of Hell and deed holder of Screams Ice Cream, Hell in a Handbasket Country Store, and its official US postal outlet. Every day anywhere from two to a hundred pieces of mail (many alimony checks) receive the official I'VE BEEN TO HELL postmark and a torching (a slight corner singeing) by the fires of Hell. On April 15 those numbers escalate substantially.

Enter the world of Screams Ice Cream through the thirty-seven-inch li'l devil door without bending over and a free cone is yours. However you do manage to get inside, though, your eyes will be immediately drawn to the genuine Transylvanian wooden coffin, where all the spooky sundae toppings sit, like bat droppings (chocolate chips), ghost poop (mini marshmallows), and buttersnot (butterscotch). Somebody must have had a fiendish frenzy labeling all those.

A Halloween gift shop adjoins so you don't have to go home without your favorite HELLUVA GOOD TIME T-shirt. Or a degree from Dam

A year-round living Hell surrounds the Transylvanian coffin sundae bar at Screams Ice Cream and Gift Shop.

U. That's right, you, too, can become an on-the-spot graduate with a major in analogy—awarded to those with great hindsight. The degree choices are limited only by your imagination, so be careful what you wish for.

There is even a wedding chapel that accommodates eight to ten people—because a marriage made in Hell has nowhere to go but up. Charges are $66, but if it doesn't last, the next one is free.

Only in Michigan do you have the choice between Hell or Paradise; thanks to a local Boy Scout troop, the round-trip mileage between the two was unmasked at exactly 666 miles. Now that's a diabolically

★ ★

unnerving statistic. Those Boy Scouts obviously have way too much time on their hands.

A novel destination spot, especially in winter when you can use your Hell-freezes-over jokes. It's not the easiest to find, though all roads from Pinckney somehow lead you here. Screams Ice Cream can be found at 4045 Patterson Lake Road, or call (734) 878-2233. Hell in a Handbasket is right next door at 4025 Patterson, (734) 648-0456. The website is as cunning as the town: www.hell2u.com.

Community Outpouring Whets the Entertainment Appetite
Jackson

You can enjoy this water park without worrying about throwing out your back or how you look in a bathing suit. Cascades Falls is a combination of dancing water, neon lights, and fast-tracked music, and has been providing family fun in the middle of Sparks County Park for more than half a century.

William Sparks, who moved to Jackson from England in 1882, had a dream of replicating a fountain he had once seen in Barcelona, Spain. As three-time mayor of Jackson, and a prominent business owner, he had the clout and money to make it happen.

Opening night drew an awestruck crowd of 25,000 on May 9, 1932. The sixteen cascading falls—five hundred feet in length with a vertical height of sixty-four feet, incorporating six fountains, 1,250 colored lights, and a 2,000-gallon-per-minute water pump—became an instant hit. Visitors worldwide came to see the largest illuminated waterfalls in North America, or perhaps to walk up the 126 steps along each side.

Time, however, took its toll on the crumbling concrete structure and renovations were seriously needed. An ambitious half-million-dollar renovation project began in 1993, and state-of-the-art equipment completed the transformation six years later.

Today, the manual operator has been replaced by a computer responsible for the falls flashing and shooting water high into the air

Boy Governor

Long before Boy George, Michigan was home of the "Boy Governor." In 1831 the governorship of the Michigan Territory was taken over by Stevens T. Mason when he was only nineteen years old!

while dancing to strains of classical music or some old time rock 'n' roll.

The falls run seven nights a week Memorial Day through Labor Day in Sparks County Park, 1992 Warren Avenue. Wednesday is family night, with additional live stage shows. On weekends there are fireworks, too. The falls are maintained by park entrance fees or by donations dropped off at the one-room Cascades Museum. The guide will be happy to fill you in on the 1920s Jackson Zouaves American Legion Drill Team, renowned for their three-hundred-steps-per-minute cadence marching with rifles. For more information check out www.co .jackson.mi.us. Stadium seating is available for 1,491.

Cell Division: Up Close and Personal

Jackson

You've pulled the Monopoly chance card that clearly states, "Go Directly to Jail—Do Not Pass Go—Do Not Collect $200." With a sallow-looking face, you drag yourself over to the doors of the largest walled correctional facility on the planet, Jackson Prison, and wait in line to be admitted by the warden. Only this time the warden is a pleasant, bubbly storyteller by the name of Judy Krasnow, a transplant from Miami who, for some inexplicable reason, was "drawn" to living behind bars here. She's the mastermind behind the Jackson

Prison tours, which will give you a first-hand feel what it's like to be incarcerated.

The experience begins behind the fourteen-foot-high turreted stone wall dating back to 1842, when the prison first opened its doors to eighty-six prisoners. From there, expansion occurred rapidly and by 1882 it resembled a mini-city, housing 3,840 inmates. Krasnow will fill you in on the historical details and macabre memories, all well-seasoned with her special dose of humor. Inside the four-story Alger Hall stands a small showcase housing artifacts such as hooks and chains and pieces of cell bars. It's here where you'll have lunch, munching on a solitary sandwich while eyeballing the high brick walls that have stories of their own. Don't worry, you can talk here, too. The infamous code of silence, prohibiting prisoners from saying even one word, was abolished in 1895.

Afterward, a trip to the basement will expand your horizons. This is where the most hardened criminals stayed in solitary cells, with ceilings and walls lined in three inches of woven steel.

Then, in a bit of an uprising, it's all aboard a school bus for a trip to Cell Block 7, closed in 2007. Yet four other cell blocks remain in operation, making this the only place where you can tour a prison while it's still on currently functioning correctional grounds. You may see prisoners out for recreational time, and since your cell phones and cameras have all been confiscated by now, there's no risk of breaching privacy.

Opened in 1934, Cell Block 7 once housed as many as 515 inmates, including such notables as former Detroit Mayor Kwame Kilpatrick and "Dr. Death," Jack Kevorkian. You'll first enter the reception area, where the murderers were separated from the check forgers. Your "greeter," aka corrections officer, will guide you to your new home. I was assigned cell #10, roughly eight by twelve feet. A few minutes of captivating stories including those about prisoners and their pet cockroaches and we were able to "escape," although not before we heard the automatic cell doors close with the heart-stopping clang you thought only existed in the movies.

Still standing strong, this "castle's" turrets kept
guard over prisoners in the 1800s.

You'll be escorted up the stairs to walk the long, endless corridors, view the showers and strip search areas, which had an incredibly artistic drawing of a Michigan State Sparty . . . all the time being mindful of the stenciled signs on every floor, NO SMOKING, NO YELLING, BEDS MADE BY 8AM.

Krasnow may give you a tour of her apartment, too, which stands inside the old prison and formerly consisted of thirty-six renovated cells. It's all part of the Armory Arts Village, which innovatively transformed the original prison into residences and artists' studios.

The tour runs about 3½ hours and begins at Armory Arts Village, 100 Armory Court in Jackson. Reservations are necessary. Tours are $35, while lunch is available for an additional cost. For more information call (517) 795-2112, contact jacksonjourneysllc@comcast.net, or visit www.judygailkrasnow.com.

★ ★

Party with Standing Room Only
Jackson

Jackson is probably not high on Bill and Hillary Clinton's list of favorite places. For it was here, under a grove of shady oaks, that the Republican Party took its first steps.

A heated July 6, 1854, saw crowds of abolitionists overflowing from a convention hall, searching for a location large enough to accommodate all the bodies, not to mention the egos. They found it in an area known as "Morgan's Forty," and began bustling under the trees for the purpose of establishing a third political party. With close ties to the Underground Railroad, Jackson was an ideal site for the group of men to pass their first resolution declaring themselves "Republicans," professing to be descendants of Thomas Jefferson's Democratic-Republican Party, an oxymoron by today's standards.

Signs designate Jackson as the birthplace of the Republican Party, but city documents are a bit more vague, recognizing it only as the site of the first Republican convention.

In 1910 President Taft dedicated a boulder on the tiny corner lot now officially known as "Under the Oaks" with a handful of tall trees and a lonely park bench.

Once considered the outskirts, today it's in the heart of a quiet neighborhood. History buffs will love it, although there's not room to do much of anything. The park is open daily; a sign says NO ALCOHOL. I guess politics in the Grand Old Party have changed.

The official Michigan Historical Marker sits at the northwest corner of Second and Franklin Street.

Hot Dogs! Popcorn! Lugnuts!
Lansing

The road to the acquisition of a minor-league baseball franchise in Lansing was covered with more than just a few nuts and bolts. It was a journey with lots of bumps for team owner Tom Dickson, who'd nurtured a passion for the sport for years. His wife, Sherry Meyers,

✦ ✦

hoping to squelch his burning desire to own a team, wondered, "Why can't you just take piano lessons?" But together the former advertising execs succeeded in acquiring a franchise with a soon-to-be condemned stadium in Waterloo, Iowa. An attempt to move their new property to Springfield, Illinois, also failed. The third try, however, was the charm when in 1995 the city of Lansing was looking for an anchor for its new downtown facility.

A name-the-team contest quickly produced more than 2,000 entries, and on May 25, 1995, thanks to Lansing resident Jackie Borzich, the Lansing Lugnuts were christened. The town was outraged, placing over 145 opposing phone calls to the mayor's office while another three hundred protests were logged at the stadium. It became a media frenzy, with David Letterman nationally ridiculing the team.

But by the time the first pitch was thrown out at what was then Oldsmobile Park in April 1996, the public had had a change of heart and was ready to embrace its Lugnuts. Fans were filling the 11,714 seats, which included the general-admission "lawn" tickets where they could bring their own picnic basket and play Frisbee on the grass. They made their team No. 1 in merchandise sales among all others in minor league baseball that year.

Watching a Lugnut game is unlike any other sporting event you've ever seen. It's nonstop entertainment with special attractions every half inning. You might be one of the lucky ones to be called on to do the chicken dance, or don a sumo wrestler's suit, or participate in the bungee run race with the Big Lug. And heads up . . . you never know when the hot dog cannon may be pointed in your direction.

Now an affiliate of the Toronto Blue Jays, the Lugnuts pull in more than 400,000 attendees a season and have already celebrated their six-millionth fan. Tickets are available online at www.lansinglugnuts.com or by calling (517) 485-4500. The seventy-game season runs from April to September. Because the Oldsmobile brand was discontinued, the park is now known as Cooley Law School Stadium. It's still located in the same place, at 505 East Michigan Avenue in Lansing.

Abracadabra

The Marshall Library had been up for sale for more than two years when Elaine Lund realized she was outgrowing her magic museum. Fearful that the historical library, completed in 1913, might become a cluster of condos, in 2000 she bought it and converted it to the Lund Memorial Library. Today it houses the more than 15,000 books devoted to magic, and she's busy working on plans to host magicians' conventions there.

What may be even more amazing is how those 15,000 books traveled from the museum to the library, a distance of an eighth of a mile. Then in her mid-seventies Mrs. Lund carried every single one of them herself ("a few at a time") and lovingly placed them on the shelves.

Open the Doors . . . Poof! Magic in the Air
Marshall

Imagine more than 15,000 books; 24,000 magazines; six hundred show bills; 2,000 handbills, heralds, and window cards; 5,000 programs; 46,000 photos; hundreds of thousands of letters of correspondence and entertainers' scrapbooks . . . all on the subject of magic. It started as the private collection of Robert Lund, containing everything magical, from the apparatus of legendary magicians to show announcements beckoning you to watch the "transformation of an orange to a lady." The oldest item, a letter defining the occult, dates back to 1584.

With nearly a million pieces in total, Lund and his wife, Elaine, decided to share their "main attractions" with the rest of the world and began looking for a home for their "American Museum of Magic." They found it in Marshall in a bakery built in 1868. Purchasing the structure, they performed their own form of renovation magic and opened their doors to the public on April Fool's Day, 1978.

Taking center stage is their tribute to Harry Houdini, with a platform filled with gadgets once used by the famous showman. You'll be able to touch and feel the renowned milk can from which he never failed to escape, including the mastodon eight lever locks used to fasten him inside. With a little prodding, you just might be able to get your guide to let you in on the secret of how it all works.

Harry Blackstone was a friend of Bob Lund's, and the museum certainly has evidence of that. His complete set of traveling cases with his orange identification markings is stored in the basement. Blackstone, whose real name was Boughton, shortened to Bouton, had a place on a lake in Colon, Michigan, referred to as Magic Capital of the World.

All in all it's a magical experience not to be missed. The American Museum of Magic, at 107 East Michigan Avenue. is open 10:00 a.m. to 4:00 p.m. Monday through Saturday or by appointment. Admission is $5.00 for adults and $3.50 for seniors and children under ten. Tours last anywhere from one to three hours and come with a money-back guarantee if you're not pleased. Call (269) 781-7570 or visit www .americanmuseumofmagic.org.

Stamp Him Prince of 49068
Marshall

Mike Schragg is not a salesman by profession, yet his constant level of enthusiasm could make anyone find exhilaration in something as mundane as a postage stamp. Which is exactly what he does, often seven days a week, as former postmaster of Marshall and founder and curator of the Postal Museum. Anything, and I do mean anything, having to do with getting the mail through is either wedged solidly into his memory bank—you can't send a human being, even if he's under the seventy-pound weight restriction; chickens are okay if they can go two days without water—or on display in the basement of the architecturally inspiring Greek Revival post office.

Mike Schragg behind the wheel of his dream
come true: a 1931 Model A Ford mail truck, now
housed in its own custom-designed garage.

A lifetime fascination with postal peculiarities came to fruition in
1987 when the museum opened its doors stocked with Schragg's
personal collection, along with donated artifacts from fellow hobby-
ists. Leather postcards, stagecoach mail pouches, old-fashioned post-
marking tools (which when demonstrated will awaken even the most
lethargic listener), and some great trivia tales are all part of the tour.

I never realized, but I'm glad I know now, that women were
responsible for the invention of home delivery. During the Civil War
they'd bombard the post office in search of letters from their loved
ones, often begging so much that the postmaster told them to leave;
as consolation he told them that if a letter appeared, he'd send someone out to personally deliver it.

Schragg's crowning glory is a 1931 Model A Ford mail truck in mint condition, which he gratifyingly chauffeurs in parades and special events, like the January 2001 inauguration of President Bush. After a 5:00 a.m. stage call, he finally rolled by the prez sometime around 4:00 in the afternoon. Patience, it's just one of his saintly qualities.

On May 24, 2008, history was made when Marshall's post office was officially named the Michael W. Schragg Post Office Building, the last year federal buildings could be named for living people.

The Postal Museum is located at 202 East Michigan Avenue. If you'd like to schedule a tour (by appointment only) or have an old set of stamps you'd like to drop off, call (269) 420-7030. Donations are appreciated.

Capital Loss Carries Over

With the length of time it takes for politicians to come to agreement, it's a wonder Michigan has a capital city even today. Detroit served temporarily in that capacity, with just about every city in contention when the final vote came up in 1847.

Lobbying was fierce and confidence was high, at least in Marshall, Michigan. The town believed so strongly it would be the permanent choice that it erected a governor's mansion, which still stands without ever having a governor in residence.

The State House had thirteen site selections before agreeing on Lansing Township, but the Senate voted fifty-one times before final confirmation. According to one account, when the last tally was taken, Marshall lost its bid by just one vote.

★ ★

"Tuba, or not Tuba"
Okemos

William White has treasured the tuba since he first started playing one when he was nine years old. Actually he began his musical career on a sousaphone, a circular tuba shaped so that one can carry it while marching. Today he's the proprietor of the Travelers Club International Restaurant and Tuba Museum. That's quite a mouthful, but then tuba players are probably used to that.

Situated in a former hardware store built in 1950, the museum-restaurant is home to more than sixty tubas, the oldest dating back to 1870. It's a horn blower's heaven with all the large bass instruments, most in playing condition, and vintage tuba photos filling the walls. Here you'll see the world's only remaining "Majestic Monster," a double E flat Helicon tuba. Even though it was built in Austria circa 1915, it's a true Michiganian, having been a fixture of the UP's Iron Mountain Community Band.

While the musical aspect will get you inside, it's the food that will keep you here even longer. For more than twenty years, White and his partner, Jennifer Brooke, have been offering guests a traveling menu. Both say they love to cook feasts of ethnic food but don't like to cook the same thing too often. Hence, the menu changes monthly, focusing on different regions of the world. One month you could be savoring the tastes of India with delicacies like lime potatoes. The next month your choice would be something with a Mexican flair. Wash it all down with one of thirty-five wines by the glass or 120 different beers.

Totally eclectic is a fitting description for the food and folly here. Don't be surprised if you see and hear members of the Michigan State University marching band come parading through at any time. It's all part of one man's devotion to the tuba. Just outside the building is White's Tribute to Tubas, an original artistic creation that honors all the "tubes" that have met their untimely demise after being run over on the field by football players. As an everlasting tribute, White

Ever wonder what a squished tuba looks like? A steamroller did the job on this one, now cemented alongside the entrance to the tuba museum.

took an old tuba, had a steamroller go over it several times, and then enshrined it in cement.

Traveler's Club International Restaurant and Tuba Museum is located at 2138 Hamilton Road. It's open seven days a week for breakfast, lunch, and dinner. Be sure to listen to the world's only Sousafountain gurgle in the outdoor patio. Phone (517) 349-1701 or visit www.travelerstuba.com for more info.

Gizzard City, USA
Potterville

"A face like a gizzard"—in Potterville that's a compliment. It all started when Potterville Days, a long-standing festival in this community of 2,100, wasn't bringing in the crowds like it used to. Recognizing the need for change, chairman Jo Lehman decided to capitalize on the No. l selling menu item since 1960 at Joe's Potterville Inn: chicken gizzards, pressure-cooked, deep-fried, and served with cocktail sauce.

Now each year on the third weekend in June, the Gizzard Festival has 16,000 waiting in front of seven vats of boiling oil for more than an hour to gobble up 2,000 pounds of digestive organs. Well, maybe not all 16,000 partake. You either love 'em or abhor 'em. It's only hearsay that they've got the same texture as a mushroom; my cholesterol can't cope with the fried part.

If you're one of those who can't get enough of the "delicacies," you're an ideal candidate for the gizzard-eating contest. Whoever can put away two pounds in the least amount of time becomes the champion gizzard guzzler (a surefire résumé booster). The time to beat is that of Brian Rock of Potterville, who in 2002 spent just four minutes and eleven seconds stomaching stomach parts, while fifteen other contestants were passing bottles of Tums.

As the Gizzard Parade passes by, everyone smiles and waves at the Gizzard Princess—there really is such a person, but only in Potterville. You have to admit the whole idea can be either humorous or repulsive, depending on your level of taste. The less adventurous gastronomes are the ones sporting the T-shirts reading WE CHICKENED OUT.

For festival information, call Jo Lehman at (517) 645-2313 or visit www.gizzardfest.com. For gizzard tasting year-round, stop by Joe's Potterville Inn, 120 West Main Street; (517) 645-2120. Six days a week they open at 10:30 a.m., Sunday, it's noon. Closing time depends on the crowd. Their new cafe is now open daily for breakfast and lunch, too. Visit Joe's online at www.gizzardcity.com.

The Covered Bridge of Ionia County

Smyrna

Michigan's oldest covered bridge sits proudly over the Flat River in Keene Township. Built in 1869, White's Bridge was named for a prominent pioneer family. Jared N. Breese and J. N. Walker took just

"If the bridge is short, a kiss will do; if it's long there's time for a hug or two." Let your imagination fill in the affairs on this 120-foot bridge.
DAVID F. WISSE

eighty-four days to construct the 120-foot-long structure. But the building wasn't without controversy. First, the people of Smyrna were short on cash, so the contract called for deferred payments—$1,000 due in 1870, with another $700 paid the following year. However, there was unhappiness over some auger holes in the planks, so $25 was deducted from the bill.

Yet the bridge stands mighty today, with only some minor repairs to the siding and a new cedar shingle roof. Otherwise, it's been in continuous use by vehicle traffic for more than 130 years.

Traditionally, covered bridges were used for a variety of happenings outside of travel, including hosting concerts, church suppers, and even weddings. Yes, the romantic aura of the covered bridge lives on today. The rough timbers provided a perfect place to carve symbols of love for all eternity.

Of course there's the popular superstition associated with covered bridges . . .

Make a wish and hold your breath as you go through. Hold it all the way and your wish comes true.

At 120 feet long, a trip through White's Covered Bridge could just make all your dreams become reality.

White's Covered Bridge stands on Whites Bridge Road over the Flat River, south of 4 Mile Road in Keene Township.

Wooden Bridges Cemented in Stone

Somerset center

Not much of the forty-two acres of McCourtie Park is visible from the street, except for the two large anemic-looking trees standing guard over the historical marker sign. Park your car, walk up close, touch the trees and the mystery begins. As you rub your fingers down the tree trunk, you soon realize that these aren't trees at all. They're really cement, and probably the best imitation of a tree you'll ever see.

A fairy-tale setting for modern-day meditation.

A brief history lesson should help clear things up. W. H. L. McCourtie (Herb) was born in Somerset Center (not to be confused with Somerset Mall in Troy, MI) in 1872. A fascination with cement, founding the Trinity Portland Cement Company, and a keen business mind in the Texas oil industry, made him millions. In 1924, he was entrusted with his family's home, which he turned into an incredible showplace, attracting the likes of Henry Ford, for some boisterous fun in his secluded underground rathskeller.

To keep his oasis a secret, in 1930 he hired Mexican artisans George Cardoso and Ralph Corona to work their magic, Using the technique *trabajo rustico* (rustic work), they applied steel frames to the house's two chimneys, and then began the tedious craft of shaping, molding, sculpting, and staining concrete to create a masterful disguise.

Their work, also known as faux bois, or fake wood, was such a success that they were then commissioned to create seventeen bridges to look like they were constructed of logs and ropes extending across the park's meandering stream. No two are alike and the whimsical works of art attract both children and adults who like to sit and ponder what life here was like long ago.

McCourtie died in 1933, leaving the Bridge Park, as it is affectionately known, to face some major changes. For a while it was home to a herd of buffalo, now completely absent. The two somewhat deserted-looking ponds were originally a swimming pool and a fishing hole stocked with trout. Today they are filled only with murky water and signs cautioning, NO SWIMMING OR FISHING. The once flourishing cypress and duralumin birdhouse still stands majestically in the original twenty tons of concrete blocks and has the capacity of housing close to three hundred purple martins.

For a period of time the park was closed for restoration, reopening in 1989. Through it all, the bridges and "trees" have maintained their youthful appearance, making it hard to believe they're over eighty years old.

* *

McCourtie Park, aka Bridge Park, with welcoming picnic tables and playground apparatus, is open all the time. You'll find it at the intersection of US Highway 12 (Chicago Road) and South Jackson Road. You can MapQuest Somerset's Town Hall at 12715 E. Chicago and it's right across the street. Call (517) 688-9223 for more information. Beware: If you arrive at dusk, there's a chance you'll witness the lady in a long blue gown who, for decades, has been seen making a ghostly appearance over the bridges.

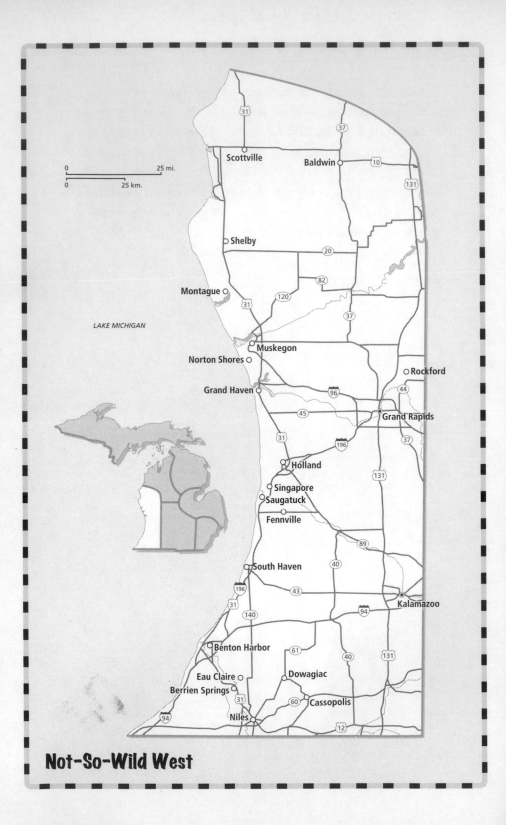

Not-So-Wild West

4

Not-So-Wild West

Chances are good you're from conservative west Michigan if you've ever worn wooden shoes while dancing in the street, or have gone to church twice on Sunday, or your first job was picking blueberries. This side of the state is true blue, with a crop that supplies 45 percent of all of blueberries consumed in America. In South Haven there's even a whole store devoted to the reported cancer-fighting brain booster. The Blueberry Store—with goodies like blueberry salsa, blueberry popcorn, and blueberry coffee—would keep a blueblood pacified for a lifetime.

The area has turned out its share of bluebloods, with President Gerald Ford claiming Grand Rapids as his hometown (he was two when he moved here). X-Files star Gillian Anderson graduated from high school in Grand Rapids, as did Jim Bakker of PTL Club fame . . . known for borrowing money. Perhaps PTL came from the words he heard even then from his teenage lenders—Pay the Loan.

Muhammad Ali has called Berrien Springs home since the mid-1970s, when he purchased an estate-sized farm along the St. Joseph River previously owned by one of Al Capone's cronies. Though he spends time in Phoenix, Arizona, too, and his three-million-dollar Michigan home has been up for sale, don't rule out spotting the Great One at the only McDonald's in town.

The picturesque sand dunes along Lake Michigan have caused a convergence of smartsy-artsy folks, so many that the Saugatuck/Douglas area has come to be known as the Art Coast with an endless stream of galleries. Where else would you find public restrooms adorned with impressionist paintings?

A worldly sampling awaits with Singapore, a once booming lumber town now buried in the sand waiting for the wind to blow just right to unveil a glimpse of a wall of chimney left behind from the 1800s. And of course there's Holland, where they still wash down the streets with their dancing feet in wooden shoes.

Michigan's west: tamed, yet curiously unspoiled.

★ ★

Tree House Stumps All
Baldwin

William Overholzer, the personification of patience and perseverance, spent twenty-two years building his home and each of the two hundred pieces of furniture in it, all out of wood. His admiration for the white virgin pine wouldn't allow him to cut any trees down, so he would row down the Pere Marquette River while his wife—his former third-grade teacher and twenty-four years his senior—looked for ideal stumps to carve.

What Overholzer did with their discoveries is almost beyond belief. A fallen tree would be painstakingly handcrafted (no power tools here) into a chair—a month's work apiece—a rifle stand, a poker table, or another utilitarian work of art. One lucky log became a rocking chair so perfectly balanced, it swings fifty-five times with only a single push. Sandpaper and glue were all homemade; instead of nails, wooden pegs became fasteners. From beginning to end, the entire process was all natural.

That carried through to the accessories as well. A turtle's shell became an ashtray. To differentiate checkers, one set was left plain, the other boiled in blackberry juice. Seventy tons of uncut stones from five Michigan counties stacked into a fireplace.

The focal point of this one-oversized-room house is a seven-hundred-pound stump. After four years of whittling away three hundred of those pounds, the stump became an incredible dining table, with drawers perfectly hollowed out for silverware. Henry Ford heard about this massive marvel and in 1940 made an offer of $50,000, only to have it rejected.

No amount of money could make Overholzer, a hunting and fishing guide, part with his beloved pines. Today his home is referred to as "Shrine in the Pines." An only child (his father was eighty when he was born) with no heirs, when he died in 1952 at age sixty-two, he willed everything to Boysville in Clinton. With the assistance of the Society for the Preservation of Shrine of the Pines, the house with the world's

★ ★

largest collection of rustic pine furniture is now open for the public to enjoy, just the way the artist and his wife always wanted it to be.

Surrounded by pines, naturally, the cabin and gift shop are located on Highway 37, two miles south of Baldwin. Tours are offered seven days a week, May 15 through October 15. There is an admission fee. For more information call (616) 745-7892 or visit www.shrineof thepines.com.

Be sure to take a walk down to the river. The setting is equally as heavenly as the "shrine."

The Old Ball Game, Now Even Older
Benton Harbor

A 1,000-member religious commune, an amusement park, and a world-class baseball team: At one time those were defining attributes of the House of David. The membership today has dwindled to eight. The train rides are long gone. But the spirit of America's favorite pastime has been given new life.

A little history lesson to comprehend the magnitude of the team that once was. Dubbed by Satchel Paige "the Jesus Boys" for their long hair and beards, the House of David ball club went into the record books for signing Jackie Mitchell in 1933, the first female professional player, who came with the unprecedented distinction of being the only pitcher to strike out—in the same inning—both Lou Gehrig and Babe Ruth. On April 7, 1930, they initiated night baseball with a game in Independence, Kansas. The guys minus the gal (she left after reportedly being asked to play an exhibition inning while riding a donkey) went on to decades of notoriety as successful athletes until the 1950s, when things started to decline and the team struck out permanently.

Baseball, though, is again on the upswing here, with the 2000 formation of a new team, the House of David Echoes, who play by pre–Civil War rules set in 1858. They use handmade, hand-sewn balls; there are no gloves, but also not as many "ouches" as you would

★ ★

**Constructed in 2000, the absence of modern conveniences
makes this new baseball stadium a remarkable venue.**

think. If a ball is caught on the first bounce, it's an out.

Vintage baseball is catching on with a number of traveling teams on
the scene throughout Michigan: the Rochester Hills Grangers, Midland
Great River Hogs, and Berrien Springs Cranberry Boggers, to name a few.

Some things don't change. A new team needs a new stadium, and
while it's not Comerica Park, the historically accurate Eastman Field
accomplishes just what it set out to do . . . take fans back 150 years,
with rustic log seating and very strict rules. Footwear at all times, no
arguing, and no cursing. Which must please the umpires more than
anyone.

★ ★

The House of David has opened up its mega-acre historical facility at the corner of Britain and Eastman for public tours, June through September, Saturday and Sunday from 1:00 to 5:00 p.m. Admission charge. Allow about two hours. For more information on tours, vintage baseball, or their vegetarian banquets, call (269) 925-1601 or log on to www .maryscityofdavid.org.

Cats Give Paws Up to Clay

LOCAL GUY SET TO MAKE MIL-LIONS SELLING CRAPPY IDEA. That could have been the foresighted headline of the Cassopolis newspaper back in 1947 when Ed Lowe fell upon a concept that was about to change the way American cats conduct their business.

As a salesman for industrial absorbents, Lowe was one day approached by a woman upset over the messy ashes in her cat's box, which caused sooty paw prints to leave their mark everywhere. He casually suggested using clay, which had a more spongelike quality. Both she and the cat loved it, and there were high hopes that others would, too.

Filling ten paper bags with five pounds of clay pellets, Lowe traipsed down to the pet store and tried to peddle them for sixty-five cents. The owner was doubtful anyone would pay that much, so entrepreneurial Lowe told him to give away the product he had hastily labeled "Kitty Litter."

* *

Gourmet Gator to Go
Berrien Springs

While most little boys had visions of growing up to become a fireman or a doctor or a rock star, Garry Zick, at the age of ten, stood up and told the world exactly what he was going to be: a sausage maker. Even in college,

Ed Lowe Industries went on to become one of those overnight successes that took decades of hard work. Always on the prowl for ways to make his goods better, at one point he built his own "cat house," employing 120 felines who were called upon twenty-four hours a day by researchers assessing their every movement.

Lowe passed away on October 4, 1995, but his wife remains actively involved overseeing their own 2,500-acre "city" replete with a church, farmhouse, and five train cars.

One more incidental . . . let's clarify those millions referred to earlier. In 1990, just before Ralston Purina purchased the company, sales of Kitty Litter were raking in more than $200 million a year. At least one tabby thinks that's not too shabby.

The Ed Lowe Foundation offers support services for budding entrepreneurs. To get all the scoop, call (800) 232-LOWE—that's (800) 232-5693. Address all inquiries to 58220 Decatur Road, PO Box 8, Cassopolis, Michigan 49031-0008. Visit them online at www.edward lowe.org.

★ ★

everyone knew him as the kid with the rows of ham and homemade sausage hanging like lanterns throughout his dorm room.

And today he's living out his dreams as owner of Zick's Specialty Meats and Sausages, utilizing the Old World techniques he learned as a kid in his dad's grocery store from German experts in the fine art of mincing meats. Desirous of a niche, he went wild—as in wild game and other exotic species—and now grinds 2,000 pounds a day into twenty-six different varieties of Buffalo Bob snacks. Except they're not all buffalo. Among the alien choices are venison, elk, ostrich, wild boar, duck, and pheasant.

More alligator goes out the door than anything else. There must be something in the taste of those scaly reptilian legs and tail that causes people's mouths to water so much they can't wait to sink their teeth into the meat and rip off a hunk.

Zick loves watching people's reactions when he offers his anonymous "try it, you'll like it" samples. When he gets the thumbs up, he owns up. You've been taken in by a bite of kangaroo.

Zick's Market has been around since 1961 and is open Monday through Saturday, except from May through September, when they close all weekend. You can view the mixers whipping up pemmican—a meat-and-dried-fruit medley second only to fruitcake—at 215 North Mechanic Street. Mail orders are available by calling the store at (269) 471-7121 or through their website, www.zicksmeat.com.

The Great Caruso Lives in Chocolate
Dowagiac

Most restaurateurs love to boast about their homemade soups, which have been simmering all day for maximum flavor. Caruso's, however, is brutally honest right on its menu—"Campbell's soup every day"—given credence by the towering stack of cans at the front door.

Whatever you think of this tell-it-like-it-is attitude, it's been a successful formula from the first day of business at Caruso's Candy Kitchen on September 22, 1922. Third generation Jane and Julie

Caruso took over in 2005. The recipes, the Italian marble soda fountain, they've passed the test of time.

The anxious anticipation I had for a taste of the olive nut sandwich I'd heard about turned quickly to disappointment when I learned that it was temporarily "out of stock." Either there had just been a mad rush or no one had ordered one in so long they didn't bother inventorying it. In any case, I guess "olive" without it.

Life is short . . . eat dessert first—no problem. Zeroing in on one of the thirty-two specialty sundaes will be, though. How do I choose between a mucky-sounding green river syrup filling a dish with crushed cherries and vanilla ice cream to resemble the Italian flag, and something called a "sauerkraut sundae"?

Maybe it'll be easier to settle on a selection from the candy case. Everything in it is homemade: chocolate pizza, chocolate toolboxes, chocolate greeting cards, chocolate cows. That's it. I'll take a milk chocolate cow to fill my dairy needs for the day.

Caruso's, with no restroom even for patrons (they have a "grandfathered" legal exemption), is in the heart of downtown Dowagiac. The 1899 building is in the middle of the block at 130 South Front Street. For hours, call (269) 782-6001.

Ready . . . Set . . . P'tooey
Eau Claire

Every Fourth of July, fans clamor for the best seat in the bleachers, slathering on the sunscreen and pulling out the binoculars in preparation to enjoy an afternoon of . . . watching people spit. A three-decade-old competition, viewed by some as the pits, others as "spitacular" . . . it's the International Cherry Pit Spit Contest. Try to say that ten times fast.

The sport grew somewhat by accident out of a seed in the mind of Herb Teichman, owner of the 160-acre Tree-Mendus Fruit Orchards, when he nonchalantly tossed a couple of cherries to some restless youngsters waiting for their parents, drew a line in the sand, and challenged them to cross over it with a hefty sputter. Give any kid a

★ ★

legitimate reason to spit and you've got a real winner on your hands.

So Teichman installed a one-hundred-by-twenty-foot blacktop court, set some rules—no foreign objects in the mouth, denture racks provided for those wishing to remove their teeth—and it wasn't long before Peter Pans from across the globe were entering the "spitting box" with all the pageantry of the World Wide Wrestling Federation. Now athletes known as Phantom of the Orchard and the Sultan of Spit sashay through the audience. But it's the opulent entrance of Rick "Pellet Gun" Krause high atop a purple Harley tossing out his autographed trading cards who really drives fans berserk. As the thirteen-time winner of the world championship, an unparalleled record in the annals of international cherry pit competition, Krause has reason to be braggadocious.

There must be a gene that determines if you'll be a distance spitter. Like father, like son. It's Rick's son, Brian "Young Gun" Krause, who holds the official *Guinness* World Record of 93 feet, 6½ inches, set in 2003.

Practice is encouraged here anytime, although the winds appear more favorable on the front qualifying court. For home use, there's the "Cherry Pitspitter Training Kit" complete with rule book, cherry pits, and an official measurement cord.

Giving pits the heave-ho isn't the only activity down on this farm. You can walk, rent a golf cart, or hop the "folkswagon" for a U-pick experience among the 10,000 trees. And don't worry about the pits. Herb has a one-ton-an-hour cherry pitter that'll do the tough stuff for you.

Time of year dictates the type of fruit. In addition to cherries, peaches, apricots, nectarines, plums, and more than 250 varieties of apples—including the one-of-a-kind apple grown in a sack—are also available. Tree-Mendus Fruit Orchards and Country Store is located on 9351 East Eureka Road. For information on tours, their rent-a-tree program, or the pit spitting contest, call (269) 782-7101 or visit www .treemendus-fruit.com.

A couple of last-minute pointers from the pros: Take a big deep breath and make sure your tongue is rolled up nice and tight around the pit for a hearty cannon effect.

Tombstone Territory

Eau Claire

"Bring back the good ol' days," exclaimed Elwell Hoyt in the late 1800s. Frustrated with all the newfangled, high-tech gadgets like electricity, the wealthy businessman decided to generate his own return to primeval times by building a log cabin devoid of any "modern" conveniences.

The twenty-five-by-thirty-two-foot structure was built without nails, and had just one window for a peek of daylight. Furniture, all

The Hoyt family will always feel right at home in this cemetery, alongside their monumental limestone cabin.

made out of coarse hickory, was kept to a bare minimum. The bed was three-cornered, brooms were made to order out of a solid stick of hickory, and no matches ever touched a candle wick, preferring, instead, a stroke of flint.

Hoyt couldn't bear the thought of parting with his home here on earth, so before he departed for good, he commissioned a tombstone to be hand-carved out of limestone and ready when the call came. (If he'd had a cell phone, the call might never have gotten through.) The monument was placed on his grave in 1905 with two "log" headstones on either side, one for him, the other for his wife, Hattie, who died in 1919.

Many a curious log cabin enthusiast has cast an eye on the Eau Claire Cemetery, which has become a regular stop on Log Cabin Day festivities.

The impact of Hoyt's thinking proves that he really was never behind the times at all, realizing early the value that it took the rest of us almost a century to appreciate. I wonder if anyone a hundred years from now will speak kindly about programmable VCRs.

The cemetery is on Highway 62, just east of the village of Eau Claire before the Highway 140 intersection. Virginia Handy, cofounder of the Log Cabin Society of Michigan, can answer any questions. Contact her at (269) 925-3836 or www.qtm.net/logcabincrafts.

Did You Know?

Michigan is the only place in the world with an annual statewide Log Cabin festival. Under proclamation of Governor James Blanchard on June 15, 1989, "the last Sunday of June of each year shall be known as Log Cabin Day."

★ ★

Do Not Feed the Animals—They're Already Stuffed

Fennville

HER NAME IS BETTY. 1930-1937. SHE LIVED IN CHICAGO. Those are the words on the sign hanging from the neck of the dog cradled in a sleigh just past the cash register at Crane's Pie Pantry Restaurant. Good thing she's near the exit door so she won't cause any folks to lose their appetite. That's because Betty is stuffed. Been stuffed for years, by the hands of a skilled taxidermist.

She may look bright-eyed and bushy-tailed,
but Betty's bark is gone forever

One of the eight full-time bakers on staff had an aunt who was awarded custody when Betty's owner died. Growing weary with the constant vacuuming she required, the aunt quickly found her mutt a new home as a curious attraction for patrons. Betty wasn't alone for long. Around the corner are a couple of Plymouth Rock chickens that apparently paid a visit to the same stuffer. If Roy Rogers could have Trigger packed for perpetuity, this doesn't seem all that unusual.

A sense of humor and an irresistible fervor for antiques have become trademarks for Bob and Lue Crane, owners of Crane's Pie Pantry. One Christmas, Lue had a tough time deciding what to buy for her husband, the man who had everything. So she decided to get him another woman and wrapped up an antique mannequin.

For years the couple had run their family's centennial fruit farm. When the restaurant opened in 1972, hours were spent perfecting Mom's pie recipe for larger quantities. Success didn't come easily, with the first batch "ending in the dumpster." But since then hundreds of pies-in-the-sky have been forklifted from the kitchen in the old hayloft down to the first-floor bakery case.

The Cranes have left no apple unturned with menu items of apple butter bread, apple butter ice cream, and apple-cidersicles. This is also the one place in the state, maybe in all of America, where you won't find any soda pop on the menu. The beverage of choice is apple cider, served chilled or hot, with free refills year-round.

The notice out back reminds us STRESSED IS DESSERTS SPELLED BACK-WARDS. Stay calm, your sweet tooth won't be tempted here by any hint of "Apple Betty."

Crane's Pie Pantry Restaurant, Bakeries, and Cider Mill are in the back of 6054 124th Avenue (Highway 89), two miles west of town. Out front sit the packing house and freezers, so don't be discouraged if you pass by. Hours vary with the season. Call ahead at (269) 561-2297 or consult their website, www.cranespiepantry.com.

★ ★

Three Tunes (or More) in a Fountain

Grand Haven

About an hour before dusk, crowds congregate in and around the Municipal Marina: locals sprawled on blankets, tourists ascending the waterfront grandstand, all anxiously awaiting the first sign of life from the Grand Haven Musical Fountain. Promptly at 10:00 p.m.—times vary according to the sunset—the throbbing percussion from *2001 Space Odyssey* vibrates through the air, followed by a booming baritone bellowing from the other side of the Grand River channel, "I am the voice of the musical fountain."

The moist mouthpiece continues, announcing the evening's playbill, *Let's Walk*. Okay, it may be hokey, but the audience loves it.

For the next twenty-five minutes, thousands of spectators feast on a free synchronized performance of light and sound with more than 40,000 gallons of water choreographed to twist, turn, and kick one hundred feet skyward with the grace and ease of a *Swan Lake* ballerina. Tunes like "Walk on By," "Soulful Strut," and "Baby Elephant Walk" are accompanied by quick color changes, set to go with the flow of the music's timbre and tempo.

When the fountain first sprouted in 1962, as the brainchild of eighteen volunteers—many of whom continue in the operations today—it was clearly the world's largest musical fountain. Leave it to Las Vegas to recently take that title away from a town with 11,168 residents. But Grand Haven's not one to rest on its laurels. Thirty new productions were added in 1997, a costly and labor-intensive project. Totally automated, one minute of water formations requires two hours of programming. Since September 2006, the public has been invited to get involved in creating software for the fountain thanks to the Grand Haven Musical Fountain Animated Choreographer.

During the daylight, it's difficult to decipher the fountain's presence on Dewey Hill, even though it's the size of a football field. It doesn't look like much of anything when it's not making music.

But for more than forty years, it's had an untarnished record of operation . . . that is, until May 2002, when a computer glitch caused the first show stoppage in history. Things have run flawlessly ever since.

At the end of each performance, landlubbers applaud and the boats in the harbor honk in appreciation and all head either home or to one of the outdoor cafes, trying to piece together the puzzle of why a man would be talking in the fountain in the first place. Seems like woman's work to me.

The Musical Fountain performs every night at dusk from Memorial Day until Labor Day, weekends during May and September.

Find the intersection of Harbor and Washington and you'll be about as close as you can get. Donations are accepted. For more information or special requests, call (616) 842-2550 or visit www.grandhaven.org/recreation/musical-fountain-schedule.

Awesome Renderings Transformed (Otherwise Known As ART)
Grand Rapids

Thinking outside of the canvas has turned a city of 188,040 into a mega-magnet for artists looking to make a differentiating mark in their field. ArtPrize began in 2009 as "a social experiment," open to any artist in the world who can find a space in Grand Rapids to exhibit.

The floodgates of creativity opened and in marched artists with the wildest of imaginations. They set up their displays on public streets, storefronts, restaurants, or anywhere else available. Walk into a coffee house and you might be greeted by a six-foot-tall shoe tree, made up of hundreds of pairs of wildly mismatched shoes.

Stroll through a three-mile radius of downtown or take the ArtPrize shuttle to nearly two hundred venues. At the B.O.B. (Big Old Building) one year you could see Glitter Girl, a photographic mosaic comprised of 50,625 sequins each independently pinned so they sparkle more with movement. "The Silverwareback Girglillas" are forks, knives, and spoons all hand placed to look like silverback gorillas.

One of 2011's top ten winners, "Mantis Dreamin'" was
created with discarded metal from an old railcar tanker.

The art may be massive, like "Mesmer Eyes . . . A requiem," an eighteen-foot-wide mosaic of more than 5,000 drawings. Or diminutive, as in "Table for Fun," where you peek inside a small hole on the side of a table to see teeny glass people, no more than a few inches tall.

The works are wacky, as in the world's largest ("Big Asstronomical") bean bag, or serious, with Beyond the Chair, a poignant piece featuring the universal symbol for disabilities surrounded by 15,000 small photos depicting the diversity of people who use the equipment.

Resourcefulness and ingenuity is the name of the game. Your mind will be boggled by what you see. It's jaw-dropping talent at its best.

In 2011 ArtPrize brought 1,582 artists from thirty-six countries as far away as Singapore, South Africa, Austria, and Argentina and forty-two states competing for what's called the world's biggest art prize. Only the viewing public has a voice in who wins, casting votes either in person or online. The top ten vote-getters receive monetary prizes totaling $450,000, with first place taking home $250,000.

In 2010, the No. 1 slot went to Chris LaPorte, an art teacher at nearby Aquinas College. His twenty-eight-by-eight-foot drawing, "Calvary, American Officers 1921," required the use of more than eighty graphite 2H pencils and between eight hundred to nine hundred skillful hours to complete his emotionally moving masterpiece.

ArtPrize takes place over a 2½-week stretch from mid-September to early October. You need to register in person to vote. Bring your patience, lines are long. For more information log on to www.artprize .org.

Square Version of the Oval Office
Grand Rapids

The first voice you hear is that of Marvin Gaye questioning through his poignant lyrics, "What's Going On?" Your words precisely. Isn't this the Gerald R. Ford Museum, paying tribute to our country's thirty-eighth president? Nothing very presidential among the Janis Joplin and Jimi Hendrix posters or the Disco Fever dance floor with flashing

The nation's first exact replica of the Oval Office exposes itself for public viewings in Grand Rapids.

colored lights. You soon realize, however, this is a 1970s overview, enabling you to become totally immersed in the sights and sounds of the era in which Grand Rapids' favorite son led the nation.

From here, you'll go through 41,000 square feet of galleries exhibiting every phase of Ford's life through attention-getting high-tech multimedia presentations. Among the expected displays, such as christening gowns and gifts to the nation, are remembrances Ford himself may want to forget: tools used in the Watergate break-in and the gun Squeaky Fromme used in her assassination attempt.

In the past, getting inside the Oval Office off-hours may have been an opportunity afforded only to White House interns. Here, anyone is welcome in the first exact replica, with its stately measurements of 35 by 29 by 18½ feet, the latter being the ceiling height. A six-minute illuminated audio presentation, rated G and dedicated to Bob and Dolores Hope, re-creates a typical day during Ford's tenure, quite different from the hypothetical X-rated version of Bill Clinton's.

Every president since Herbert Hoover has been the recipient of his own museum and library, although Ford's is the only facility that's split. His library sits miles away in Ann Arbor on the campus of his alma mater, the University of Michigan.

Attractively situated on the west bank of the Grand River in the heart of downtown at 303 Pearl Street Northwest, the Gerald R. Ford Museum, including the Gerald and Betty Ford burial sites, is open every day except New Year's Day, Thanksgiving, and Christmas. Admission charge. Call (616) 254-0400 or visit www.fordlibrarymuseum.gov.

President and Vice President without One Vote

Michigan is the home of the only person to become president of the United States without ever being elected either president or vice president. Gerald Ford of Grand Rapids was appointed vice president on December 6, 1973, when Spiro Agnew resigned the position after pleading no contest to income tax evasion.

The next year, on August 9, 1974, Ford took the oath of office of the president, replacing Richard Nixon, who left the White House over the Watergate scandal.

da Horse da Vinci da Signed
Grand Rapids

Milan—Grand Rapids—Milan. It's a trip that took five hundred years for Leonardo da Vinci's horse to complete. Today the world's largest bronze horse sculpture has taken up permanent residence in the Frederik J. Meijer Gardens and Sculpture Park, while its identical twin is an Italian citizen.

Put out to pasture for more than five centuries, da Vinci's horse now strikes a statuesque pose in Meijer Gardens.
TRAVEL MICHIGAN

A little background will help . . . In 1482 da Vinci was commissioned by the duke of Milan to create the grandest equine statue ever known. A big assignment, resulting in twenty-five years of work. (Cut him some slack; he had other projects, like completing *The Last Supper*.) Finishing touches had just been put on the three-story-high clay model when war broke out, and the French invaders found great pleasure in using it for target practice. The creative genius died in 1519, lamenting on his deathbed the loss of his cherished steed.

That would have been the end of the story, but in 1967 da Vinci's thumbnail sketches of the horse miraculously reappeared. To see the project through to the end became the mission of pilot and part-time sculptor Charles Dent, but then he, too, died, and many thought the animal was jinxed.

An article in the *New York Times* prompted Fred Meijer to step in, vowing to do whatever he could to make da Vinci's dream come true. The third time was the charm, with artist Nina Akamu supplying the interpretation that resulted in the twenty-four-foot-high, fifteen-ton, Renaissance-style *American Horse*. Out of the same mold, now broken, came the *Il Cavallo* (*The Horse*), standing in Milan, Italy.

Visitors from Italy come to Grand Rapids, and vice versa, to try to detect the subtlest of differences, of which there are none. Except the Italian stallion, on its marble pedestal, stands six feet closer to heaven than the American in the courtyard of the Meijer Gardens, accessible for a "mind-expanding" touchy-feely experience. Do you think perhaps they're receiving vibes from da Vinci signaling approval of his now completed work?

The Frederik Meijer Gardens and Sculpture Park is found at 1000 East Beltline Northeast. It's open 362 days a year; closed Thanksgiving, Christmas, and New Year's. Get in touch with them at (616) 957-1580 or (888) 957-1580, or visit their website at www.meijergardens.org.

Admission charge for adults and children over two years of age.

Tulips Beheaded for Two Lips

In Holland, Michigan, tulips are not to be taken lightly. As a matter of fact, they're not to be taken at all. If for some odd reason you feel the sudden urge to run up and pick one of the six million that blossom each spring, it's a $100 fine.

In May 1998 Eric Balcazar found out the hard way that the city is serious about the penalty. Just before Tulip Time—the third largest flower show in North America, drawing more than a million people—the twenty-year-old was accused of beheading not just one, but as many as 2,000 tulips.

Love may be blind, but a photographer wasn't. During Balcazar's trial a picture showed up in court of his girlfriend, smiling broadly, with none other than a tulip clenched between her teeth. Admitting that he clipped the 'lips (but only 975 of them) to impress her, his unlawful expression of affection cost him $740 in restitution, twenty-five days in jail, and eighty hours of community service.

Holland District Judge Hannes Meyers Jr. divided the sentence: fifteen days behind bars immediately, the remaining ten during the next year's Tulip Time. Hoping that the hours of community service would be spent planting bulbs for the city, Judge Meyers also issued an official advisory: From now on, "tiptoe through town very carefully."

Paddle Pops

Holland

No matter where I go in Michigan, it seems every town has some kind of food that locals insist I have to try before my visit is complete. Such was the case regarding the Holland, Michigan, paddle pop. And the

★ ★

place to pick a paddle pop is the Holland Peanut Store. Investigative journalist that I am, I had to comply.

Although they've been doing business at their current location since 1954, the Fabiano family has been in the chocolate business since 1902. And they're still making goodies in a family way. It seems everybody in the store is a brother, sister, aunt, or uncle. Now, you'd think that a family that is a chocoholic's Valhalla would have members approximately the size of one of the windmills that dot the area, but that's not the case.

Mary (Fabiano) Stille, one of the sisters who helps run the business, says the answer is moderation. Moderation may be the family's motto, but it doesn't seem to apply to the customers. Apparently it's not uncommon for people to walk out with more than $100 worth of goodies. "If they didn't, we wouldn't be here," chirps the barely-a-size-2 Stille.

The store also does corporate orders for gift baskets and jars of assorted nuts, which make up a big piece of the business, but it's the individual sweet tooth that carries the brunt of the load.

You're probably thinking, "It's great reading about a family-owned business that's been around all that time, but what about the paddle pops?"

There's a method to my madness. If I'd told you about paddle pops in the first paragraph, your mouth would've started watering, and chances are you'd need a chocolate "fix" more than you'd need to know about the Fabiano family and their Dutch treats. It's kind of like making you eat all your vegetables before you have your dessert. But you've read this far, so here it goes.

A paddle pop is a huge slice of ice cream with a "paddle" stuck in the end. It's then painstakingly hand-dipped in homemade chocolate, not once but twice; but the real secret of paddle pop perfection is the way the chopped peanuts are lovingly roasted before they are wrapped around the chocolate-covered confection.

Is ice cream on a stick alone worth a drive to Holland? Absolutely not. That's why I recommend you justify it by buying about a dozen

★ ★

paddle pops to take home and stick in the freezer. Think of it as doing your part to conserve our precious fossil fuels.

The Holland Peanut Store is at 46 East Eighth Street; call (616) 392-4522. Open Monday through Saturday. Hours vary with the season.

Clomping to the Beat

I've always had tremendous respect for members of marching bands. Playing an instrument is tough enough, but doing it while you're marching in time and trying to form a giant kumquat in a "Salute to Salads" boggles my mind.

The Holland High School Marching Dutchman Band, however, not only plays, marches, and makes formations, but also does it in unforgiving wooden shoes. Walking in wooden shoes is tough enough; marching in them should require a purple heart from Dr. Scholl.

It turns out the secret of marching in wooden shoes is "socking it to them." The 150 band members wear, on the average, about four pairs of thick wool socks inside the wooden shoes that they purchase at Holland's Dutch Village. Although Dutch dancers in Dutch costumes carrying the Netherlands' flags have replaced the traditional majorettes, both drum majors do their high-stepping in their lumber loafers.

Band director Charles Boulard, who had directed the band since 1980, hung up his wooden shoes in 2009. During his tenure, he'd shepherded his wooden-shod flock to the 1985 presidential inaugural parade, the 1995 Tournament of Roses parade, the January 1, 1998, Disney World Main Street parade, and every year in the Holland Tulip-Time Parades. Current band director Jonathan Bogue says he'll continue the tradition of wooden footwear while he leads his musicians in their theme song, "Tiptoe through the Tulips."

★ ★

Cougars and Tigers and Bears, Oh My—Yes, and They Really Do All Fly!

Kalamazoo

A zoo where cobras and camels fly? It really does exist. It's the Kalamazoo Air Zoo, a 100,000-square-foot hangar packed with more than seventy of the world's most remarkable aircraft. These were the wings that played a major role in our country's preservation of peace in World War II, the Vietnam War, and the Persian Gulf War.

The "zoo" fulfills the dreams of Pete and Sue Parish, both pilots who served in World War II. Opened in 1979, their menagerie includes a Wildcat, Bearcat, Hellcat, Tigercat, and Sue's own Curtiss Warhawk P-40. It's this aviation wonder that stands out with its pink (make that desert pink) exterior and painted trimmings of lipstick, eye shadow, and the longest lashes this side of Betty Boop. A one-seater, it has an assigned crew weight of 120 pounds, perfect for Sue, who continued to fly her own plane . . . when she was eighty years old.

Always in expansion mode, it's now become the world's first museum-meets-indoor-amusement-park themed attraction. In addition, it's home to the Midwest's only 4-D, 180-degree theater, where you can experience the excitement of being dropped into the middle of a World War II bombing mission. State-of-the-art flight simulators and other indoor rides complete the opportunity to totally escape, even if just for a few minutes.

It's hard to miss the eight-hundred-by-thirty-two-foot "Century of Flight" hand-painted mural, the length of which is comparable to three football fields. It took fourteen months to complete and at one time held the *Guinness* World Record as the world's largest indoor mural.

In October 2011, a 50,000-square-foot expansion was added with even more interactive activities, including the historical "Space: Dare to Dream" and a special exhibition featuring the women of aviation.

The Kalamazoo Air Zoo is also home to the Michigan Aviation Hall of Fame and the Guadalcanal Memorial Museum. Visit them at 6151 Portage Road. An admission fee is charged. Open seven days a week;

★ ★

hours vary with the season. Call the museum at (269) 382-6555 or (866) 524-7966, or visit www.airzoo.org.

White Sails in the Sawdust

Montague

One of the weather vane commandments declares, "Thou shalt have 1 inch of weather vane height for every one foot of roofline." At forty-eight feet tall, the world's largest weather vane needs a roof the size of the Mackinac Bridge.

Instead, the hand-formed aluminum breeze barometer, created by Whitehall Products—which just happens to make more weather vanes than anyone else—found a home on the corner of Dowling and Water Streets, its second residence. The first was a sawdust-filled peninsula—the result of the lumbering era—where the 4,300-pound structure stood or tried to stand for fifteen years. Not pulp fiction, the weather vane, with its eleven-foot-tall ship topper, was sinking in the sawdust. Its only chance for survival was to be landlocked.

Speaking of sinking ships, that's exactly what the crowning glory of the vane represents: the Great Lakes lumber schooner *Ella Ellenwood*. Home-based on nearby White Lake, the *Ellenwood* ran aground eight miles north of Milwaukee during a perilous storm in the fall of 1901. The crew abandoned ship, but the blustery winds blew the ship apart, leaving no remnants until the next spring, when a section of the ship's nameplate, bearing the word ELLENWOOD, was found in White Lake. By the grace of Neptune, it had drifted all the way across Lake Michigan, returning to the exact spot it had taken off from. Who says you can never go home again?

You can verify the nameplate's existence at Montague City Hall, where it's permanently displayed.

The fully operational weather vane, at last check, was standing in town at 8718 Water Street and on extremely windy days has the ship doing 360s faster than an exorcised head. All weather-related and unrelated questions can be answered by going to www.cityofmontague.org or calling (231) 893-1155.

One Man's Junk Mail Is Another Man's Fortune

Indirectly you can blame Niles, Michigan, for all those catalogs crowding your mailbox and email. Perhaps if eleven-year-old Aaron Montgomery Ward had been happier here while earning twenty-five cents a day working in a local barrel factory, he might never have been inclined to start the country's first mail-order business. In 1872 he sent out a single page offering 162 items for sale with a "satisfaction or money-back" guarantee. When he died forty-one years later, Montgomery Ward had annual sales of $40 million.

Sub Performs Multiple Life-Saving Operations
Muskegon

The rising-sun decals on the bridge silently speak volumes. Thirty Japanese ships sunk; fourteen others damaged. The record of the USS *Silversides,* now sitting in Muskegon's Pere Marquette Park, gives it the distinction of being the most successful surviving wartime submarine.

The "Lucky Boat" appeared to have been blessed from early on. In December 1943 George Platter, fireman second class, watched as his personal bombshell fell, a gangrenous appendix in need of immediate removal. What do you do in the middle of the ocean with no one on board who's ever performed an operation? That's when Pharmacist Mate Thomas More stepped in, with galley knife in hand, executing his first appendectomy on the officers' dining table. Six days later, after toppling out of his rigged-up bunk during a death charge, Platter returned to active duty. The account lives as perhaps the most celebrated seafaring surgery of all time.

★ ★

As you walk the 312-foot distance through half a dozen entries no bigger than eighteen by thirty inches, a tour of the *Silversides* enables history to come alive. Anecdotes galore provided by your guide will keep all ages entertained. Like the story of the captain's dog, Admiral, who made it through four months at sea—albeit illegally—to return home in need of a little fire hydrant education.

Torpedo Man Third Class Mike Harbin was the only man to die on board—on May 10, 1942, hit by enemy fire. Unsubstantiated reports of haunting noises and furnishings that have mysteriously moved suggest that Harbin's ghost remains lodged inside.

You can check all this and more out for yourself by spending the night on board *Silversides*. There's room for seventy-two guests in four cramped quarters. (You'll get to know your neighbor really well.). USCGC *McLane* accommodates another thirty-eight. Guests are mostly youth-oriented groups, but anyone over the age of five is welcome. Book early . . . there's up to a year's wait for weekends. Weekday rates run $30; weekends, $35, meals not included.

The Great Lakes Naval Memorial Museum (at 1346 Bluff Street), including the USS *Silversides,* is open April through October. Times vary for the hour-long tours, and a fee is charged. Call (231) 755-1230 or log on to www.silversidesmuseum.org.

Doggie Drive-Thru Becomes "Pawsible" Reality
Niles

All customers here are chauffeured up to the drive-thru window, where they paw the counter and then stick their heads out the window—literally barking out their orders as loudly as possible. It may seem like crude, animalistic behavior. That's to be expected, since all the patrons are animals of the four-legged variety.

It was no April Fool's joke when former nurse and hospitality manager Maggie Patterson unleashed the world's first pet drive-thru on April 1, 1990. (The attention she received that day certainly didn't hurt—the *National Enquirer* and CNN gave her "a billion dollars worth of free publicity.") Canine convenience food—a McDonald's for animals—is serious business, and catering to man's best friend's every whim, whine, growl, and squeal is her main objective.

Menu items are all hand-made of top-quality ingredients in the Patterson kitchen, yielding gourmet goodies that Fido can really sink his teeth into. What pampered pooch wouldn't love to take a bite out of an eight-inch-round doggie pizza—rolled dough smothered with cheese—or chow down on a burger with molasses fries? It's all natural and all healthy food, with no-fat, no-sugar cookie options for the diabetic dog's diet. The pain of turning another seven years older in just twelve months is eased with a party pack, complete with a single-layer cheddar birthday cake, frosty paws, and a party hat.

Hungry cats, horses, llamas, pot-bellied pigs, and the occasional pet rat also find their way to the drive-thru, keeping Patterson busy as the only employee, baking and serving more than fifty pounds of flour-based treats each week.

Full pets are happy pets. Full, clean pets are even happier. Hence the addition of the U-Wash Dog Wash, a private shower with professional hair blowers to prevent owners' pet peeves of clogging the drains at home.

Patterson also offers personalized nanny service for canines in her home, with plans to expand her growing one-stop shopping enterprise to nearby Granger. The Doggie-Drive-Thru, 2639 South Third Street in Niles, is open Wednesday through Saturday. Call Maggie or any of her own three dogs at (269) 683-7511. Remember, July 28 is National Drive-Thru Day.

Tree Branches Out in Song
Norton Shores

At first glance the Christmas tree is most impressive, with perfectly shaped branches shooting out from its sixty-seven-foot-tall frame. A second look may raise an eyebrow or two. Are those people among all the layers of greenery? Yes, your eyesight is fine. What you're looking at are 240 students from Mona Shores High School, a school which, since 1985, has provided the key ingredient in the Singing Christmas Tree.

In these days of political correctness, America's tallest singing Christmas tree bravely branches out to represent a public school system, and the community embraces it wholeheartedly. More than two hundred volunteers dedicate round-the-clock service to assembling the 850 pieces of unistrut steel, similar to working with a giant "erector set."

Lighting and decorating an eight-story tree could be a disaster waiting to happen. Not here, though, where more than 15,000 linear feet of electrical wiring runs to more than 25,000 colored lights. Then more than 5,200 linear feet of festive greenery imported from Germany is lovingly "fluffed" prior to placement of the "stars."

Getting more than two hundred excited teens to silently ascend in total darkness isn't easy. They scale steep "ladders" on either side and scooch into their assigned place. The whole process takes six to eight minutes, during which time spotlighted soloists and a quartet entertain the audience. Then the set goes dark and the Christmas tree comes to life, literally.

Accompanied by a full orchestra, the celestial bodies, dressed in spic 'n' span sailor outfits, burst into song. (Appropriately, the school, located on the shores of Lake Michigan, has a sailor as its mascot.) The sound is magnificent, engulfing the body and soul of the entire audience.

The school's choir has become so popular that it's outgrown the fifteen-tier tree. With more than three hundred members, they all can't fit inside, so freshmen stand below providing the skirting. The angel on the top is naturally the place of honor and is awarded to the student who has conquered an exceptional challenge. Otherwise, places are assigned according to seniority. Except for the "tree monkeys," as the dedicated parents affectionately call themselves. They surround the back of the tree, out of sight, and are there for moral and physical support, offering water and assistance to those who have difficulty standing during the hour-long program. Emergencies are handled by several nurses on site and a fireman suspended in a harness.

Look carefully: The tree ornaments are really 240
living, breathing, and singing teenagers.
RADIUM PHOTO

★ ★

Of course it can be mighty warm up there under the lights. A fan helps by constantly blowing cool air throughout—unless you were in the tree the day one student couldn't overcome his nausea and lost his Christmas cookies right into the center of the fan. The air wafting through wasn't heaven scent.

Shawn Lawton has been the choir director for over a decade and waves his glow-in-the-dark batons (basically Maglite flashlights with an attached piece of plastic) from a balcony sixty yards away. Admittedly, he suffers from a fear of heights and has never ventured to the top of the tree himself. Just keep him away from the fan.

The multitalented choir performs an eclectic mix of Christmas, Hanukah, and African music the first Thursday, Friday, and Saturday of December. Tickets to the sold-out "you must see it to believe it" experience go fast. For more information call Mona Shores High School at (231) 780-4711, ext. 8319. Or check out the Frauenthal Center for the Performing Arts, a 1,700-seat movie "palace" built in 1929; www .frauenthal.info or (231) 722-9750.

And the Wiener is . . .

Rockford

Where can you go for four hours of work and be inducted into a hall of fame? Try starting out at the corner bar. Not just any corner bar, but the one and only Corner Bar, the oldest building in the town of Rockford, where people put their stomachs on the table for a chance to be inducted into the Hot Dog Hall of Fame.

The rules for membership are simple: Eat twelve hot dogs with at least the special chili sauce, developed by a former Army cook at Prohibition's end, in one four-hour sitting and you're a wiener! Your name goes up on the wall alongside the other 5,000 in the fellowship. Extra credit can be earned by consuming twenty or more—then the dogs and an official congratulatory T-shirt are on the house.

Established in 1965, people from all over the world have gone into the "hall," with the most recent grand championship awarded on

Thousands of sensible people and millions of loaded
hot dogs have found their way to this wall of fame.

December 5, 2005, to Balinda Gould, a forty-one-year-old mother of
one. She guzzled down forty-three chilidogs in less than four hours to
beat the previous record of 42½ set by Sharon Scholten Van Duinen
of Kentwood back in 1982. For her efforts, Gould received $500 and
had to call in sick the next day with a screaming gall bladder. In March
2006, professional competitor from New York City, Tim Janus, ate
43½. But he's a member of the International Federation of Competi-
tive Eating (yes, there really is such a thing) so he eats for a living,
unlike the rest of us who are supposed to eat just to live.

Words of advice for potential applicants who are thinking of mustering up the courage to catch up on the record: Eat something small beforehand so your stomach is in the expansion mode, and make sure you bring enough cash. One young man recently was pumped up after devouring a dozen in two and a half hours, only to be deflated when he discovered he couldn't pay his bill, forcing him to chow down another eight so his total consumption would be complimentary.

The chili dogs are $1.99 a piece, and even if you don't succeed, you can buy a hall of fame T-shirt. Your friends back home won't know the difference. The Corner Bar with its novel take-out window is on the corner at 31 North Main Street. Call (616) 866-9866 or visit www .rockfordcornerbar.com.

The Eighth Wonder

Some call it the eighth wonder of the world. St. Frances de Sales Parish of Muskegon is one of the few places large enough to house Norton Shores' Singing Christmas Tree. Designed by internationally acclaimed architect Marcel Breuer in 1966, the church's north and south walls are ninety feet high, with the roof held in place by the pressure of the east and west walls forcing against it. It's an optical illusion that the west end of the ceiling appears to be higher than the east end.

Materials used for the church's construction include 7,000 cubic yards of concrete weighing 14,000 tons, with 575 tons of reinforcing steel embedded in that concrete. To see it for yourself stop by 2929 McCracken (231-755-1953) or visit www.sfnortonshores.com for a virtual tour you'll never forget.

Formica, Neon, and a Basket of Fries
Rockford

Diner (*Dye-ner,* n.): A restaurant in the shape of a railroad dining car.

Throwbacks to the 1940s, most diners are long gone now, yet oddly enough you can find a trio of the neon flashers sitting on Highway 57 in Rockford. What Diana Ross did for the Supremes, Rosie's is doing for Dinerland: holding everyone together while getting ready to branch off to stardom on her own.

Baby boomers may well remember Rosie's diner for the Bounty paper towels commercials featuring Nancy Walker as Rosie the waitress. Well, this is the authentic "quicker picker-upper car" where all those spots were filmed, now plunked between two other oldies, but goodies, just like her, only not as famous.

Purchased by artist Jerry Berta in Little Ferry, New Jersey, and transported in two sections—"four days, ten flat tires, and one fire"—Rosie

Rosie's shiny exterior got its start as the Silver Dollar Diner in 1946.

arrived safely in Rockford. An instant success in 1991, only five years later she honored her one-millionth customer.

Time has taken its toll on Rosie; and even though she's still open for business, her once glistening stainless exterior looks a little worn. Her two sidekicks never did much on their own. One of them is now an ice cream parlor. And the quirky miniature golf out back with hot dog and hamburger sculptures? It's still there, on the agenda for renovation.

As of 2006, Jonelle Woods is the new owner and she's working hard at restoring it all to its former glory. Let's hope the hula-hoop onion rings keep gliding across the Formica while we hear Rosie's juke-box blasting Gloria Gaynor's "I Will Survive."

Rosie's is located on 4500 14 Mile Road (Highway 57). Open seven days a week. Hours vary with the season. Call (616) 866-FOOD—that's (616) 866-3663—or visit www.rosiesdiner.com.

A Brassy Bash? Send in the Clowns

Scottville

Here they come, just a stumblin' down the street, playing a down 'n' dirty, bump 'n' grind version of "The Stripper." These are the men of the Scottville Clown Band, two hundred members strong, with wailing trumpets and clarinets blasting out blues that would stop a crowd from drinking on Bourbon Street.

It's been that way since 1903, when musical merchants dressed down in their weekend worst to entertain customers. A wide cross section of professions fills today's roster: Doctors, teachers, truck drivers, school band directors, a judge, and a blacksmith are among those packing up their instruments and heading to Scottville, dubbed the "Clown Town," for seventeen rehearsals a year. Each a superbly accomplished musician, the end result is hundreds of performance requests and skyrocketing sales of CDs.

Led by a hobo with a toilet plunger for a baton, the "bums" take their penchant for fun as seriously as they do their music. Individualized band uniforms range from the ridiculous to the sublime . . . one

**Miss Piggy, aka Fred G. Lyons, marches to his/her own
beat, hoping not to lose an eyelash.**
KATHLEEN T. LOWLOR

wears a tutu and tights with a C-clamp for an earring; another is a
Miss Piggy look-alike. And occasionally "groupies" will filter through
bearing signs, WILL U MARRY ME?

The bonds of friendship and camaraderie provide impetus while the
serious side of their nonprofit organization raises funds for musical
scholarships statewide. All costume, travel, and general expenses are
paid out of each member's personal resources, making the convivial
clowning "a very expensive hobby," worth every penny.

Their annual "world tour," comprised of fifty play dates, doesn't
always result in their typical post at the rear end of the parade. Often
in demand is their "clean socks and shorts concert," categorically a far

more formal affair with a sit-down audience and maybe a bow tie or two sprucing up the baggy pants, hula skirts, and silly hats with arrows shooting through their heads.

It tickles the heart to know that more than a hundred years hasn't changed one thing . . . the sound of laughter from the crowd is always music to these bozos' ears.

The best place to get the entire scoop is from their website at www .scottvilleclownband.com.

A Gem of a Friend to Men

Shelby

The idyllic backdrop for a fairy tale, crystal-clear gems the size of pearl onions adorn the state's royalty: Miss Michigan, the Cherry Queen, Mrs. Asparagus. Surprise, it's only make-believe. Not the royalty part. The jewels; they're fake. The manufactured product of the Shelby Gem Factory.

Winding through streets in the small town of Shelby, at the end of a lonely industrial parkway, you hardly expect to find such authentic-looking "rocks" engineered inside the rather nondescript-looking building.

The birthplace of more gemstone products than anywhere else in the world was conceived in 1970 by Larry Kelly, who grew up next door in Hart and didn't see any reason to leave. After all, the necessary chemicals are shipped in from the four corners of the earth, and you really don't need to inspect the gems in person to make a purchase. If you see one diamond, you've seen them all, each an exact clone of the next, varying only in shape and size. Same goes for the rubies, emeralds, and sapphires that come off the assembly line.

The secrets of Hollywood stars—rumored to be more than a few— remain hidden inside; company policy forbids disclosure of the names of anyone who has opted for a "falsie."

Some odd requests have been made over the years—like the woman who had bone removed from her foot, then requested the knucklebone be set with a "Shelby gem" to be worn as an anklet. A

At fifty carats, even Elizabeth Taylor would have required more than one finger to hold this ring upright.

retired plumber in search of that special "drip" coming down from his golden faucet found it in a pear-shaped diamond. The record, though, goes to the man who bought the biggest multifaceted stone ever custom-created—a forty-carat insert for the center of his steering wheel.

The insurance industry put the kibosh on their factory tours, but the theater runs a video of the whole process. A hands-on faceting machine gives everyone the chance to experience the grunt and grind of the gem cutter's life.

At $150 a carat, regardless of shape, these diamonds in the rough could just be a guy's best friend.

Shelby Man Made Gemstones is located at 1330 Industrial Drive; (231) 861-2165. Open fifty-one weeks a year, Monday through Saturday; or visit them online at www.shelbygemfactory.com.

Finally, a Hotel That's Right on Track

South Haven

Only really big news makes the front page two days in a row. The arrival of not one, but two raging red cabooses in South Haven met that criterion for the local newspaper nearly twenty-five years ago.

What began as an innocent southern Illinois business trip for Bob Burr ended up in the purchase of "a little something" to bring home to his wife, Pat—a pair of tail-end train cars. (She might have been just as happy with a four-slice toaster.) Fanfare and hoopla never seen before in this resort community greeted the newcomers' arrival at their humble abode on the site of the out-of-service train depot.

And there they sat on abandoned tracks until people started asking "if their kids could spend the night." Before too long, grown-up kids wanted to rest their head on a piece of railroad history, too. So the Burrs renovated both interiors (leaving the privacy of the conductor's loft intact), added screen porches, and baptized them "The Caboose Hotel."

Train buffs and those who simply favor "detachment" start dialing on April Fool's Day to put in their reservations. By the first of May, both cars generally are filled for the next five months. Pat, who spends her days with a mop and Lysol in hand to keep the "twins" spotless, may be the only person who can't wait to see the autumnal equinox. That's when both she and the rails shut down until the following spring.

Open April though October, the hotel's rates in 2011 were $139 during the week, $169 on weekends for double occupancy. During the fall, prices drop to $99 and $139.

The air-conditioned cabooses sit on the tracks at 162 Dunkley Avenue. Directly across the street is the Burr's latest acquisition, the former coal station, also available for nightly rentals. To reserve a spot in either location, call (269) 637-8492 or visit www.oldharborinn.com. They're now handling reservations for the Burrs (since Bob's now the mayor of South Haven).

Pinkie Playground

5

Pinkie Playground

Originally this chapter *was titled "Frozen Cherries," but it was modified partially to remain in keeping with the symbolic image of the shape of the hand, and also so as not to rock the tractor of the vast number of cherry farmers in southwest Michigan. How prophetic that alteration proved to be. Several years the cherry crop bit the ice, forcing replacements to be flown in from out of state for July's National Cherry Festival in Traverse City.*

So "Pinkie Playground" will hold. There's no disputing this area knows how to have fun 365 days a year, no matter what the weather. With the best snow skiing in the Lower Peninsula joining sunbaked shores of crystal-clear lakes, put two of anything on your feet or arms and it's "instant party." Venture out to the sandbar on Torch Lake and you'll see a conglomeration of two-legged and four-legged species hankering for a knee-deep walk on water. Or sail away to new heights in the state's only hang gliding near Frankfort.

Party animals are ubiquitous with a moose that slops kisses in a local tavern, an island that's gone to the birds, another dedicated to beavers, a whopper of a fish story, a cow that's been pinched and pulled in every direction, and an eighteen-foot grasshopper a wee bit too stiff for the bar-hopping scene.

And in this chapter I'll take the wraps off the secretive whereabouts of the preeminent tourist value: totally free and guaranteed to humor the stuffiest curiosity seeker.

Put Another Nickel in the Nickelodeon
Acme

In 1904 the only sounds you heard from the building were moo. Today the site of this former 180-acre dairy farm echoes with the sounds of hundreds of mechanical instruments. It's heaven for those who may not have taken their piano lessons seriously, since all the instruments play by themselves.

A lofty Amaryllis you never have to water, with a thirty-foot carved façade and a musical repertoire of 2,200 dance tunes.

* *

The Music House Museum opened its doors to the public in 1983. Founded by five private collectors who recognized that only 3 percent of all mechanical instruments still exist, it now is home to items from more than two hundred individuals.

And what you'll hear through the corridors of the "barn" is musically inspiring. All instruments have been fine-tuned to work as they did years ago. You can drop a nickel in the 1917 Cremona piano nickelodeon and hear an authentic honky-tonk version of "Jingle Bells."

Time hasn't altered the sound generated by the incredible reproductive talents of a 1925 piano especially built for Detroit auto magnates Mr. and Mrs. Fredrick Fisher. Thanks to the magic in the perforated paper rolls, you'll enjoy a private concert by twenty-six-year-old George Gershwin playing "Rhapsody in Blue." Yes, it'll be exactly as he played it, note for note, with all of his personal artistic expression.

Long before there were DJs, there were dance organs, and one of the grandest of them all fills the museum's loft. The Amaryllis from the Victoria Palace Ballroom in Belgium was built in 1922 and has the same vigorous reverberation that it did during those Roaring Twenties.

Check out the world's largest music box, built by Regina, which plays discs that are a far cry from the CDs of today, measuring a whopping twenty-seven inches in diameter.

The prized Conover "Giraffe" piano arrived to thunderous applause in 2011. A vertical grand piano, it stands somewhere between ten and twelve feet high, and may have been the transitional instrument between the harpsichord and the piano. It's great for people with limited space, and really high ceilings.

It's a stroll down memory lane with everything set in historically accurate vignettes, from the general store to the Hurry Back Saloon.

The Music House Museum is at 7377 US Highway 31 North. It's open May 1 through October 31, as well as weekends November through New Year's. Contact (231) 938-9300 or www.musichouse .org.

★ ★

Bloomers Butcher America's Only King
Beaver Island

A remote island, thirty-two miles north of Charlevoix, improperly labeled Beaver Island (there are no beavers; a cartographer came up with the farfetched idea that the island is shaped like one) is the backdrop for America's only kingdom. James Jesse Strang, an attorney who became self-appointed royalty—a redundancy in some eyes—founded a Mormon settlement here in 1847.

With a couple of thousand followers, he went about setting laws of the land best suited to his personal desires. A flamboyant personality

Strike Any Chord— No Tune-Up Needed

"Timbre, more timbre, quick!" Words from Frank Youngman spoken to the logs and brake drums filling his backyard that have grown to be music to his ears. One night the self-described musical activist was dropping wood on the fire when he heard tunes popping from the pulp and the lightbulb went off. Why not create a garden of sound using nature's own as the instruments? Seemed so obvious, and it sure beat showing up somewhere as old drywall.

A teacher by trade, he approached a professor at Central Michigan for permission to do an independent study project with the "final" a concert in the forest. A stepladder of various-sized branches became a xylophone. Other twigs, hung clothesline-style, play the musical scale. As for the brake drums, they add dulcet tones unmatched by earthly creations. All instruments are left as they were innately tuned by that Goddess of Good Vibes somewhere in the sky.

with an eye for the ladies, worn out from disguising his polygamous wife as his "male" secretary, he issued the ruling that church elders must all have two simultaneous marriages. Not a popular edict with the women, especially his first wife, who packed her bags and headed to Wisconsin.

That didn't discourage Strang, who hastily acquired five wives and twelve offspring. Unhappy with long skirts on gals, bloomers (less material, more leg) became mandatory dress, with those found in noncompliance publicly taken to the whipping post. Well, that did it. The troops were riled enough to take action into their own hands and, in 1856, two bloomer busters shot and killed the only man who would ever be king in America.

Youngman passed his exam with soaring sounds and continues to hold spontaneous jam sessions with fellow members of the "Log Rhythms," but all are welcome. No experience or training is necessary, as long as you can get past the unusualness of the presentation and are willing to cast your musical inhibitions to the wind.

Cadillac has embraced its maestro of the woods, hiring him as artist in residence for their Michigan Community Partnership Program. Expect soon to hear and see people of all ages marching to the beat of their own drummer.

The award-winning Sound Garden project has expanded to the downtown area of Cadillac at the Clam River Greenway off Chestnut Street. For more information contact the Cadillac Area's Visitors Bureau, 222 Lake Street, (231) 775-0657 or (800) 22LAKES, or access their website at www.cadillacmichigan.com/soundgarden.

Youngman has plans to upgrade his own garden by sawing a bowling ball in half to serve as giant log caps. In his spare time he's a member of the Jive at 5 Swing Band.

With only 551 permanent residents at the last census, two hundred departing in winter, Beaver Island is home to more wildlife than anything else. A two-hour ferry ride from the mainland transports tourists to another world, a tranquil setting with fifty-four miles of beaches to stroll without a single pair of bloomers in sight.

Contact the Beaver Island Chamber of Commerce for information on accommodations and to learn more about the wild St. Patrick's Day celebration: (231) 448-2505 or www.beaverisland.org.

Homes from the Stone Age
Charlevoix

These cottages are so delightfully quaint, you fully expect to see Snow White waltz through the front doors with Sneezy, Dopey, and Sleepy trailing close behind. They're affectionately known as the mushroom houses, because that's what they resemble with their curvy, slanting cedar shake roofs, irregular chimneys, and round stone walls. The Disney behind the scenes was Earl Young, a man as fascinating as the homes he designed.

Born in Mancelona, Michigan, in 1889, he moved to his beloved Charlevoix at age ten. Neither an architect nor a builder but for sixty years a licensed real estate broker, Young was simply in love with rocks and wanted to share his enthusiasm with the rest of the world by designing imaginative homes, reflecting the beauty of the area.

In the 1930s his work incorporating the stones of Michigan into livable spaces began. Fieldstone, local quarry limestone, boulders, Onaway limestone, even red stone barged over from the Soo Locks—they're all represented.

A portion of the celebrated homes, including the backless half house, sits in a triangle on Clinton, Grant, and Park Avenue. Young, a diminutive man barely standing five feet tall, built the home at 306 Park for himself. It's scaled to his size, filling out only eight hundred square feet; word is that an average-sized adult isn't able to stand up straight in the four-legged bathtub.

Residents dish up the "fungus among us" in the mushroom houses.

The remainder of the unique and pricey "hobbit" homes (some have sold for upward of a million dollars, although the recent economy has changed things) are in an area known as Boulder Park, near the Charlevoix hospital. They're a must-see trademark of northern Michigan. Maps for self-guided tours can be obtained from the Charlevoix Chamber of Commerce at 408 Bridge Street. Contact (231) 547-2101 or (800) 951-2101 or visit www.charlevoix.org. A precious few are available for weekly rentals; call (231) 547-6480. The Charlevoix Historical Society occasionally gives tours of many of the homes; contact them at either www.chxhistory.com or (231) 547-0373.

The Never-Freezing Story Pro-crasti-nator's

Paradise . . . that's what an aquatic section of Cadillac could be called. If you need a sure bet excuse for avoidance, simply say you'll do it "when Lake Cadillac, Lake Mitchell, and their connecting canal all freeze over." It's not that this area's supersensitive to global warming; the point is that no matter how low the temperatures go, these three have never frozen over at the same time.

Back in the days of lumbering, when "log on" meant a fallen tree made it to the barge, the Clam Lake Canal was built as a convenient passageway, and for as long as anyone can remember, early each November it turns to ice. No surprise there. About a month or so later the lakes on either side chill out, and that's when the unexplainable happens . . . the canal thaws. As hard as they may try, no one's been able to figure out why this trio just can't get in sync, but it's a fact that will easily fill in any blank moment at your next cocktail party or will prevent you from being sent away as "the weakest link."

Michigan's Shape Prehistorically Predestined
Charlevoix

Michigan may have been mapped out long before any cartographer got involved. A nine-ton limestone boulder is the centerpiece of the fireplace in the main dining room at the Weathervane Restaurant. It's not just any large stone that's filling space, though. If you look closely, it's in the shape of the Lower Peninsula of Michigan, complete with highway markings. Yes, that does appear to be Interstate 75 running through the middle and US Highway 131 on the left, with Highway 23 to the right.

The restaurant is another example of Earl Young's infatuation with stones. Once a gristmill, Young bought the place and began his conversion. He got rid of the top two floors and replaced them with a roofline patterned after a gull's wing. The exterior was faced with limestone and Onaway stone from the local quarry. Then he found his

Eighteen tons and what do you get? An imposing fireplace serving as a map of Michigan.

★ ★

prized "mapping" boulder in 1954 while building roads in Charlevoix. Using a heavy-duty crane to lift it through the roof was itself a remarkable feat.

What may be even more astonishing is what Young placed it on: a meteorite weighing the same as the massive boulder, a whopping nine tons. It's mind-boggling to think that both are identical in weight, yet the meteorite is only a quarter of the keystone's size.

Stafford's Weathervane Restaurant is located at 106 Pine River Lane and looks like one of Young's charming mushroom houses on steroids. Hours vary. It's best to call ahead: (231) 547-4311. Check out the website at www.staffords.com/weathervane.

Continuing Saga of Cherry Pie Debate
Charlevoix

Because alphabetically Charlevoix comes before Traverse City, the cherry pie debate that starts there will continue and, hopefully, end here.

Some facts not added in part one regarding the Charlevoix cherry pie pictured with this story:

First, it's a monster heavyweight, topping the scales at seven tons.

Ingredients for the pie crust alone were almost beyond comprehension: 850 pounds of flour, 325 pounds of water, fifteen pounds of salt (not blood pressure–friendly), 110 pounds of milk (local cows really put out for this one), 375 pounds of shortening, and fifty-five pounds of baking powder.

Just in case you may want to create this for your next family picnic, the recipe for the filling includes 4,950 pounds of Michigan cherries, 2,850 pounds of water, 260 pounds of butter, ninety pounds of tapioca, 3,850 pounds of cherry juice, 540 pounds of sugar, 120 pounds of lemon juice, and another ninety pounds of salt.

Top the crust with an egg wash and sugar. In this case, that was done by helicopter.

One lonely piece of pie has been waiting here since 1976.

Then bake in a fourteen-by-eighteen-foot oven for five hours. Let cool before slicing (may take anywhere between two and four days).

While this pie was never authenticated by *Guinness* (like the pie in Traverse City), in 1976 it was dubbed the "world's largest pie in the USA" (not sure exactly what that means . . . maybe the world was smaller then).

The Charlevoix pie pan sits at 6591 South US 31, right in front of the Fire Department's Station #2. (See part one of the Great Cherry Pie Debate listed under Traverse City.)

★ ★

His Passion for Pumpkins Can't Be Squashed

Frankfort

The bigger, the plumper, the rounder, the better. That's how Ed Moody prefers his models. Size really does matter to him. His discriminating taste seeks out only natural beauties who tip the scales over 1,000 pounds. And don't be surprised when he stumbles upon the perfect creation to hear him exclaim his favorite pick-up line: "Hey, pumpkin, want to come home with me?"

Moody is possessed by pumpkins, at least during the month of October when he takes time off from his day job as Grand Traverse County's electrical inspector to pursue his passion for pumpkin carving.

Since age five, when he was cutting out triangle eyes on jack-o'-lanterns, his talent has grown, so that today he turns monster squash into masterfully crafted works of art. For years he had dreamed of carving Cinderella's carriage. He found his nirvana in the garden of Traverse City's Phil Wolinsky, with a four-hundred-pounder he named Corina (after the song). The carriage has now become Moody's trademark, and each year fans clamor to observe him sculpt an even larger pumpkin so they can put their real-life princesses inside for a picture.

Every fall Moody visits weigh-offs throughout Michigan in search of pleasingly plump pumpkins, be they white, grey, green, orange, yellow, or blue. Growers now donate their produce in exchange for his "cut-up" demonstrations and the return of the seeds inside, which can sell for a hearty $5.00 each.

After the pumpkins are transported via trailer and hoisted by crane onto Moody's front lawn, he delves into his tool box, reaches for a simple paring knife ("nothing works as good as a four-inch paring knife"), and spends the next three to four hours transforming the fruit into everything from whimsical creatures adorned with earrings made of #4 ground wire, to an almost-life-size PT Cruiser.

Moody loves what he does and can proudly recall the weight of every pumpkin he's ever carved. A typical Halloween will find seven

★ ★

Standing more than four feet tall, this scary sculpture represents some of the more than 11,000 pounds of pumpkins Ed Moody carves each year.

tons of fun perched outside his door, attracting more than 1,000 trick-or-treaters. Not bad for a town with a population of 1,500.

For premium pumpkin pleasure, plan a visit to 722 Leelanau Avenue in Frankfort the week before Halloween (50,000 others do). That's when the carvings are in their prime. For more information you can visit Moody's website, fittingly found at www.pumpkined.com.

Acres Aweigh

It was 1957 when Mary Lou Morse's thriving honeybee business saw its big plans for expansion fall through the cracks. While the Eastport Inn was being trucked across a frozen Torch Lake, horrified crowds watched as the ice gave way and the building took a nosedive. Miraculously the inn was recovered and remains alive and well today on the site of Brownwood Farms—makers of the yummiest cherry butter in northern Michigan.

Anyone who remembers the Brownwood Farms Restaurant in its heydays of the 1960s might want to check out old photos of the singing waitstaff, known as the "Honey Bees," for one of the group's more recognizable alums, actress Christine Lahti.

The Brownwood Country Store sits just off US 31, three miles south of Eastport and three miles west of Central Lake on East Torch Lake Drive. For more information call (231) 544-3910. For all the gourmet foods, check out www.brownwoodfarms.com or call (888) 772-9444.

If You Don't Like Cherries . . . Please Press 6

Glen Arbor

Apples-schmapples . . . peaches-schmeaches . . . oranges-schmoranges. That's what one northern Michigan store thinks of those. In fact before you go through "customs" here, you must "declare all bananas." It's pretty obvious when you enter the Great Hall of the Cherry Republic that the only fruit that matters in life is the cherry. Sweet or tart.

★ ★

Bob Sutherland is the mastermind who started it all in 1989 by selling cherry festival T-shirts from the trunk of his car. Two years later he introduced a food product, Boomchunka cookies, a colossal oatmeal cookie "booming with cherries and white chocolate." And let's just say his business boomed from there.

At last count, there were 174 different cherry products, ranging from cherry salsa, cherry tortilla chips, chocolate covered cherries, cherry wine jelly, cherry pepper jelly, cherry vinegar, cherry salad dressing, cherry tea, cherry coffee, cherry ginger ale, cherry candles, and

Where cherries reign.

cherry body lotion, to republic wafers, the world's only cracker with dried cherries baked inside. All products are made locally with Michigan cherries, two million pounds of them a year to be exact.

Only now they're being sold out of a spiffy three-building compound. The Great Hall, constructed in 2004 of materials from northern Michigan, is the largest. The timber is from Suttons Bay. Employees handpicked all the stonework from a quarry in the UP. It's here you'll get a taste of the Cherry Republic, literally. You can almost make a meal on the plentiful samples. The company says they give away $60,000 worth of free samples annually, including sips of their own award-winning cherry wine.

Anything you buy at the store is subject to an added refundable 1 percent tariff, which will be donated to agriculture programs in the state.

You can have a full cherry meal next door at the restaurant, where Friday night barbecues attract five hundred people feasting on ribs marinated in cherry wine and vinegar and glazed with cherry BBQ sauce. For dessert, there are fourteen different varieties of homemade cherry ice cream.

All 225 employees cheerfully love their cherry jobs. The company motto says it all: "Life, Liberty, Beaches, and Pie." Make that cherry pie.

Open seven days a week, the Cherry Republic is closed only on Christmas Day. You can't miss the SPIT PITS HERE sign at 6026 South Lake Street. For more information, or to request a catalog as 500,000 others have done, call (800) 206-6949. If you don't like cherries, you'll be instructed to press 6, and you'll be promptly disconnected. Visit them online at www.cherryrepublic.com, where they have their own Glen Arbor webcam.

There are now stores in Traverse City, Charlevoix, and Ann Arbor, but none of them have the regal flair of the Great Hall.

Best Formed Body in the Country

Michiganians can brag all they want about our state being Mother Nature's best achievement, but when national TV makes that claim, then the case is finally settled. In August 2011, ABC's *Good Morning America* held a competition for the most beautiful place in America. After hundreds of thousands of votes were cast, the winner was Northwest Michigan's Sleeping Bear Dunes National Lakeshore, with its sixty-four miles of Lake Michigan shoreline. Get ready to feel the sand of the majestic glacier-formed dunes for a first-hand experience of the most gorgeous spot in the entire United States. Who's going to argue with anything on TV?

Flicks Flash '50s Fun
Honor

"Back to the Past" could be the name of a feature film shown at the Cherry Bowl Drive-in. It's definitely a blast back to the '50s and the way things used to be.

First opening its screen in 1953, this outdoor movie theater is proof that some things have never changed. Like the popcorn popper— it's the original, still kicking out perfectly popped kernels, with real melted butter. The sound system remains the same, with vacuum tube motiograph amplifiers, still sitting on posts that light up red when the movie starts. (If you prefer, an FM radio option has been added that allows you to hear everything through your car's own stereo system.)

★ ★

This drive-in's quirky exterior hasn't moved a muscle since the '50s.
DIANA NOWAK

The earliest projectors remain on the premises, although they've been replaced with upgrades to state-of-the-art equipment.

The singing of "The Star Spangled Banner" before every showing as a tribute to our servicemen and -women remains a long-standing tradition.

Double features are standard fare nightly, accompanied by an introduction, cartoons, a vintage clip or two, and the obligatory intermission, allowing for a trip to the concession stand. The movies are all first run, but they never show anything stronger than PG-13 or any movie that glorifies teen driving or drug use. Occasionally "characters" will show up beforehand, possibly from *Pirates of the Caribbean* or *Godzilla.*

Owners Laura and Harry Clark bought the Cherry Bowl in 1996 from Jean Griffin, who started it all way back when. Only two owners in all these years. Now it's Harry's booming voice that can be heard coming out of the loudspeaker announcing birthdays, followed by a chorus of three hundred honking car horns.

Hula hoop contests, a children's playground, a dog run and—of course—a '50s-themed miniature golf course round out the package of wholesome family fun.

Cherry Bowl Drive-in sits at 9812 Honor Highway. It operates seven days a week, "rain or shine, dusk is the time." Call (231) 325-3413 or go to www.cherrybowldrivein.com for more information. Right next door is the Cherry Bowl Gifts and Goodies (same owners), open year-round.

25 Miles in Three Minutes or Less
Ironton

Talk about a shortcut. The Ironton Ferry has been saving people miles of driving, either by car or by horse, since 1884. Lake Charlevoix is shaped just oddly enough so that to get from one side to the other you have to drive either twenty-three miles one way or twenty-seven miles in the other direction. Or you can take the ferry to cross the 620 feet of water.

The current *Vessel Charlevoix,* the official title designated by the Coast Guard, has been sailing since 1926. It makes trips from 6:30 a.m. to 10:30 p.m. seven days a week, mid-April to Thanksgiving, weather permitting. There's no schedule. When someone shows up, the boat leaves. Captain Robert Curtis shuttles more than 71,000 cars a year on the "two-and-three-quarter- to three-minute" trip. He says on his best eight-hour day, he carried 435 cars. With a capacity of four cars, that's at least 109 crossings.

Totally self-supporting, the fifty-foot ferry has managed to keep rates much the same as they've been for years: $3.25 per car, fifty cents per person without a vehicle or bicycle. One slight exception: In 2002 the price of transporting a bike went from fifty cents to $1.00.

Over time the Ironton Ferry has had its share of the limelight. During the mid-1900s Captain Sam Alexander made it into *Ripley's Believe It or Not* for traveling 15,000 miles without ever being more than a quarter mile from his home. Yes, he lived next door to the boat launch.

The ferry is operated by the Charlevoix County Transportation Authority and is located about six miles south of Charlevoix on Highway 66. Call (231) 547-7200. For the latest info, go to www.charlevoix county.org/transport.asp.

A Home Worth Bottling Up
Kaleva

"Bottoms Out" was the commanding cry that Finnish immigrant John J. Makinen issued his troops in the early 1940s as they fastidiously lined up 60,000 glass bottles. Your first thought might be, "Not very effective armor." That's where you're wrong.

As owner of Northwestern Bottling Works, somehow he stumbled upon the insulating properties of the glass he was manufacturing. Taking to heart the old expression "People who live in glass houses shouldn't throw anything away," the biggest recycling project Kaleva has ever seen started to take shape. Makinen decided to build his own glass house, cutting off the tops of already defective bottles, cementing them with his own secret-recipe mortar, thereby creating the exterior four walls.

Makinen died before he could move in, but it must have been a happy home nevertheless. Says so right on the front, the words are one of several artistic expressions bottled throughout.

The Bottle House became a museum in 1980, operated by the Kaleva Historical Society. There's nothing special about the interior, a

**The homeowner may have given up $6,000 of bottle
deposits for the ultimate in insulated walls.**

standard three-bedroom home. But the artifacts are entertaining, as is
the commentary by society representatives. President Brian Smith provided the missing piece to the puzzle of the century . . . why we in the
Midwest don't call them "soft drinks" or "soda" like the rest of the
country. It was the "pop" of the cork out of Makinen's bottles that's
never left us.

In 2008 the museum purchased the largest collection of Makinen
Tackle Company lures and memorabilia, all produced in Kaleva during
the 1940s by Bill Makinen, whose father built the house.

Other home-grown Kalevans include Ella and Lila Wigren, who
went on to become nationally known as the Tony twins (you may
remember those dreadful smelling home-permanent kits of the 1950s
and 1960s), and Darth Vader, more familiar to some as the voice of

★ ★

CNN, James Earl Jones. Smith ends our tour by asking, "What would Ella Fitzgerald's new name be if she married Darth Vader?" Don't think too hard.

You can examine all the bottles with their raised-lettering insignia KALEVA anytime at 14551 Wuoski Avenue at the corner of Kauko. There are limited hours to eye the inside: Memorial Day through Labor Day, Saturday and Sunday only, noon to 4:00 p.m., Saturday only through the end of October. Other times by appointment. Call (231) 362-2080.

Insect to Inspect . . . Closely

Kaleva

Why is a grasshopper, ten feet high, eighteen feet long, weighing five hundred pounds, standing guard at the Kaleva Centennial Walkway? In a roundabout way, to pay homage to the Finnish settlers' patron saint, St. Urho.

The Legend of the Farmer's Nightmare states that it was St. Urho, with his mighty pitchfork, who chased all the grasshoppers out of Finland, rescuing the vineyards from their throes of destruction. Truth be told, grapes don't grow in Finland. The story arrived here via Minnesota, and how trusting can you be of a state whose governor once said he wanted to be reincarnated as a bra?

But the myth served as impetus for Brethren High School Service Learning and Manistee Intermediate School students to create their own version of the giant crop killer, in exact proportions, out of 100 percent recycled metal. The big bug's nose in another life cooked someone's dinner as a Weber grill, its legs are old railroad spikes, and the scales on its neck were once shovel faces.

Under the direction of Wellston's Andy Priest, the project has met with huge community appreciation. Dedicated on March 16, 2000, the feast day of St. Urho, there's not been one sign of grasshoppers infiltrating the area. My guess is, they're attacking the vineyards of Minnesota at this very moment.

This artistically perfect grasshopper, known as the
Farmer's Nightmare, was built entirely by local students.

To see if any part of the grasshopper once belonged to you, take
Wuoski Avenue to Walta Street. Turn left, look right, and you'll spot it.
The Kaleva Historial Society now maintains the grasshopper. Call (231)
362-2080 or visit www.kalevami.com.

That Fish Was How Big?

Kalkaska

Here lies a whopper of a fish tale . . . seventeen feet long, twelve feet
high, more than 320 hours to reel it in. This account isn't fiction. The
fact is, those are the statistics of the National Trout Monument.

The trout spouts, twists, and shouts—all under colored lights.
THE LEADER AND THE KALKASKIAN

Constructed in 1966, the work of art commemorates the passage a year earlier of a bill declaring the brook trout as Michigan's official state fish. Those trout bite big in Kalkaska, which has been the home of the National Trout Festival since 1935.

A local grocer, Leo Nelson, had dabbled in some animal sculpture previously and wound up being the one selected to turn out the finished product. Like many artists, he chose to work with his model au naturel: an actual frozen trout.

The fisherman's shrine showcases Nelson's masterpiece emerging from a fountain of colored lights. With mouth wide open, the fidgety fish appears to be leaping for the fly—that is, if the fly's still there. Through the years youngsters have had a good time zipping up the trout and nimbly tackling that fly.

Either way it's a striking tribute to the trout, and it turned out to be the start of a second career for Nelson. Soon afterward, he got his chance to really bring home the bacon, so to speak, when the state of Iowa commissioned him to sculpt a giant thirty-foot pig.

Catch the National Trout Monument right in the middle of town on Cedar Street, aka US 131, aka Highway 72, aka Highway 66. For more information call the Kalkaska Chamber of Commerce at (231) 258-9103 or check online at www.kalkaskami.com. The trout festival has its own website at www.nationaltroutfestival.com.

The Great Pyramid of the Forty-Fifth Parallel
Kewadin

In the middle of almost nowhere, between a dirt road and a fruit orchard, stands a twelve-foot-high pyramid. Rather than a tribute to King Tut, it's a shrine of sorts to the generally unrecognizable Hugh J. Gray. Hugh who? Gray . . . that's the color of most of the boulders cemented neatly together in 1938.

The attached plaque identifies Hugh Gray as "the Dean of Michigan Tourist Activity." In reality, he was a founder of one of Michigan's early tourism associations and someone, somewhere, must have thought this would be a fitting tribute to him.

There are several reasons why it's worth venturing off the main roads to see it. First, it's made up of eighty-three stones, one from each county in the state. It's fun just to see what may be lying beneath your own home. Each stone is chiseled with its county name, except for Wayne and Muskegon Counties—they're identified with large, raised metallic lettering. There are some real beauties. And then there are some that may raise an eyebrow or two. Wexford County is represented by a totally black chalky rock that has attracted more than its fair share of tourist graffiti.

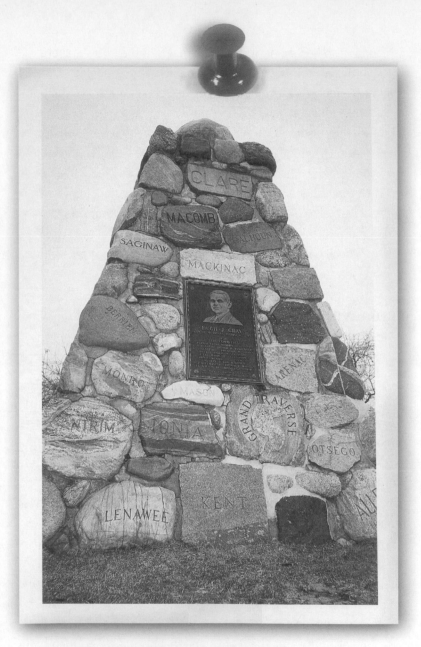

Step right up for the best view in Michigan.

Second, when you're here, the pyramid tells you, "This point is half way between the equator and the North Pole." It sounds plausible. Yet just a few miles north there's a similar sign that identifies that spot as the 45th parallel. You be the judge.

Finally, when you stand in front of the pyramid and turn to the west, you'll be witnessing one of the most beautiful views of Grand Traverse Bay. From a visitor's perspective, Gray really knew what he was doing.

This quirky monument in itself has achieved some notoriety. It's pictured prominently on the front of every bottle of Cairn Side Juice, a 100 percent pure cherry juice manufactured in neighboring Elk Rapids.

With some good detective work, the monument to the Dean can be found, appropriately enough, on Cairn Highway. From US 31, take Ames Street in Elk Rapids four miles east to Cairn Road (the Oasis Tavern is on the corner of Cairn and Ames). Turn left on Cairn. Head 1½ miles north. You'll see the pyramid on your right.

Not a Fish Tale . . . It's Honestly the World's Biggest
Kewadin/Torch Lake

When it comes to fishing, exaggeration is the name of the game. Not so, though, in October 2010, when a real whopper of a salmon was caught on Torch Lake in northern Michigan. So big, it set a world record for land-locked Atlantics, tipping the scales at twenty-six pounds, twelve ounces. Prior to that, the all-tackle world record took the hook in Sweden in June 2010 weighing a mere twenty-four pounds, eleven ounces.

Matt Supinski, a fishing guide from Newaygo's Gray Drake Lodge, was responsible for leading Indiana cardiologist Tom Aufiero to the shallow end of Torch's turquoise blue waters at the Torch River Bridge where they spotted the monster. Using a six-pound test line, the beauty fought for over fifteen minutes, performing a series of acrobatic jumps and twists before succumbing to the net.

The International Game Fish Association officially certified the record the following March, after requiring the scale to be calibrated for accuracy.

The Michigan Department of Natural Resources wasn't surprised by the super-sized female, saying that Torch has a reputation for growing colossal lake trout and muskies. Not long before, someone caught a twenty-nine-pound brown trout.

Unfortunately, the MDNR stopped stocking Torch with Atlantic salmon in 2006 due to budgetary cuts. However, since the monster record-setter was thrown back in, alive and kicking, there's still a chance you can catch her again, after she may have even added on a few pounds.

If you're interested in help landing your own world record, Matt Supinski can be reached at Grey Drake Lodge and Outfitters, 7522 S. Gray Drake Bluff in Newaygo; (231) 652-2868; www.graydrake.com.

Costumed Carrier Creates His Own Caribbean

Mancelona

It's not often that mail carriers ever achieve rock star status. Yet in Mancelona, a town of 1,408, that's just what has happened to Patrick Mizgala. A jovial guy with a unique sense of humor and a style that could be described as a cross between Jimmy Buffet and Santa Claus, he's turned his day job into a lifetime of fun.

As an auxiliary rural carrier, he doesn't have the strict uniform requirements of the United States Postal Service. So he's infused his work with his own signature style. Decked out in one of his typically outrageous Hawaiian-print shirts with wild plaid shorts, he gets people to smile—even when he delivers a bundle of bills. Mizgala says he's always dressed that way and has never cared if his clothes matched. His wife, Theresa, creates his flamboyant fashions, adding long-sleeved fleece when the weather cools.

It's not just his clothes that make him stand out in a crowd. He tools around his route in a 1975 authentic postal Jeep, refurbished in his own inimitable design. Painted green, red, yellow, blue, and orange (all five of the OSHA safety colors), he proclaims his vehicle is easy to spot in the frequent snowstorms and proudly adds he's never had an accident. A gangly pink flamingo gawks at motorists from the left-hand side mirror.

Patrick Mizgala creates a new definition of dressing for success.

Mizgala's unconventional "mail" image may make Ralph Lauren or Gucci cringe, but the folks on his route love him. Kids think he's the ice cream man. Dogs happily line up for treats. And almost daily people ask to be photographed with him. Thanks to the Internet his celebrity has spread—his picture has been spotted on the website of a fan in Arkansas.

Patrick and Theresa Mizgala live in the heart of Mancelona. They're easy to find. Patrick's brightly colored mail vehicle sits outside, and chances are their home is still the only one on the block whose front lawn is adorned with a frolicking flamingo.

Antiques Are the Apple of His Eye
Northport

Antiques: Items that become more valuable with age, including food.

Surprisingly, even edible products increase in value with time. John Kilcherman and his eighty-five acres of vintage apples are living proof. A third-generation fruit farmer (his grandfather tilled the land here in 1884), his orchards now are home to two hundred different varieties of antique apples.

Kilcherman, who admits he "likes anything old," defines an antique apple as one with origins dating way back in time. Currently there are 14,000 known varieties, most of them with unusual shapes and some curious names. You might get a blank stare if you ever walked into a grocery store and asked for a pound of Snow Wolf River, Jelly Crab, or Sheepnose apples. But that wouldn't be the case at Christmas Cove Farm, where those are all readily available in season.

Demand for the historical fruit has grown so much that Kilcherman and his wife, Phyllis, now have a mail-order business, shipping a medley of Winter Banana, Green Pippin, and Mother-in-law ("really tart") all across the globe. Each comes with a description of its heritage, like the Seek-No-Further pink and gold apple dating back to the early 1800s. A good dessert, it got its name because it "tastes so good that you have to Seek-No-Further."

Antiques are almost an obsession here. While the apples are a fall-time business, Kilcherman works year-round on his bottle collection. He claims to have the world's largest antique bottle collection, numbering more than 10,000, housed in his 2,000-square-foot pole barn. They're all neatly arranged alphabetically on floor-to-ceiling shelves and protected by a nearly-invisible wire so that they won't fall during a big wind or when they're dusted.

Strung overhead is every sort of tin can of yesteryear. Yes, he collects those, too. Hundreds of them. Old potato chip cans, Crisco cans, cherry pie filling cans, and pails that once housed beef brains and pork brains.

A true venture c-apple-talist.

Everything is open for the public to view September 15 to November 15. "It's a sight to see." And there's no charge "to look and go away." But you won't want to miss tasting the homemade cider or an antique Opalescent or Bread-and-Cheese apple.

Kilcherman's Christmas Cove Farm, one of the few antique historical apple farms in the United States, is appropriately located at 11573 North Kilcherman Road. Call (231) 386-5637 or visit www.applejournal.com/christmascove.

If the Tree Fits, Shoe It

You're driving along US Highway 131, Highway 66, just north of Kalkaska, when you notice a confounding sight on the east side of the road. You blink once, then again, attempting to clear your focus, hoping to identify the seemingly foreign objects lacing a wide-spreading tree. What at first appears to be a cluster of brightly colored birds turns out to be none other than hundreds of pairs of shoes embodying the souls of the branches in a nest of high-heeled spikes, sneakers, and boots. Each twosome appears to be as gently strung as if it was a Christmas ornament.

Yet it's not a special occasion that causes these heels to kick up the bark: It's an everyday occurrence that commenced with the first sighting in January 2001. Mystery abounds with nary a hint of whom or what concocted the idea of the anomalous growth. Whoever is responsible for the botanical bombardment is certainly not a loafer. He's been busy through the years, surreptitiously adding to the mounting number of leather and canvas footwear suspending from boughs. And faithful footwear it is. After one blustery windstorm a fallen branch was seen lying on the ground, still clinging to its inseparable sole mate.

The puzzling shoetree has been the source of controversy, with all eyes on the lookout for the perpetrator. Since the hangings appear to be nothing more than harmless fun, state police say they won't tie themselves into knots trying to horn in on the shoe sower's territory.

Where old soles come to rest.

Occasionally the tree requires some thinning out, like the time someone heaved a giant pair of waders onto one of the branches. Heavy duty shoes weigh too heavily on the arms, causing a potential danger to motorists. For the most part, though, all the footwear appears to be hanging in its final resting place.

Exclusively for Bird's-Eye Viewing
Northport

Should Alfred Hitchcock ever decide to drop back down from that great moviemaking set in the sky to direct a sequel to *The Birds,* the stage has already been set and the actors are all in their places, though not necessarily ready to go. Thousands of herring gulls and cormorants have been nesting on a five-acre island just off the shores of Northport since the beginning of time, and it's a safe bet their tail feathers aren't going to move now.

The island has been a source of trouble for years. Suffering from an identity crisis, it's universally referred to as Gull Island, but when first purchased in 1853, it was Trout Island, then Bell Island, Fish Island, Fisher Island, and Bellow Island, the official name.

Edward Ustick became deed owner in 1910 and got down to the arduous task of building his family's dream cottage. The birds did their darndest at trying to stop the invasion of their territory, but in a struggle to win this survival-of-the-fittest challenge, there are stories of Ustick dynamiting the aviary. Feathers flew, but the birds remained and the home with its creative plumbing—one pipe laid across the island, entry at one end, exit at the other—served as a summer retreat until 1942. Ultimately it was a group of young Northporters, now grown residents in the area, who entered through an open window and vandalized the entire property.

Remnants of the house remain—actually only two chimneys, both visible from shore with a good telescope. Everything else has weathered away, except one tree and, of course, the birds. They remain victorious over man and island.

In 1995 the Leelanau Conservancy purchased Gull Island for the purpose of continuing research, which so far hasn't turned up any news as to why the birds chose this landmass over others. But no one's going to take it away now. The stench is repugnant, and even when investigators make it ashore, cormorants have been known to bombard right through at least one guy's cap, drawing blood. Hard

★ ★

hats are now a necessary fashion accessory in this modern-day version of Gilligan's Island that's really for the birds.

The Leelanau Conservancy can be reached at PO Box 1007, Leland, MI 49654; (616) 256-9665; or www.theconservancy.com.

Ice Doesn't Freeze Out the Faithful
Petoskey

On a clear summer day, you may be able to catch a glimpse of the white marble crucifix that's submerged in twenty-five feet of water off Little Traverse Bay. Or you could wait until midwinter when thousands make the trek to the cross over the ice.

Either way it's a spiritual experience for many and an incredible story to all. It began in 1962 when a father from Bad Axe ordered an eleven-foot, one-ton crucifix from Italy for his son's grave. It didn't survive the overseas voyage without damage, so it was refused and eventually offered for $50 in an insurance sale. Purchased and restored by the Superior Marine Divers Club of Wyandotte, the statue was submerged in Grand Traverse Bay on August 12, 1962, as a shrine to all divers, living and deceased. It's believed to be the only underwater crucifix in the Great Lakes.

During the placement, the right arm cracked, broke off, and was taken home by one of the Wyandotte divers for safekeeping until it could be repaired. But before the repairs were made, the diver passed away. So his widow was left holding the right arm of Jesus. She turned the appendage over to Ron Tocco, a fellow club member and avid photographer, who had been part of the original underwater expedition.

In the meantime Dennis Jessick, a young, energetic diver from Harbor Springs, became the new caretaker of the shrine. Determined to find a way to offer landlubbers an opportunity to experience the underwater shrine, he waited until the frozen H2O was at least a foot deep. Then he painstakingly spent hours with a chain saw, carving out two six-foot triangles as observation stations. In 1986 the First Annual Ice Viewing of the Underwater Crucifix was held, running from 10:00

a.m. to 10:00 p.m. Jessick says nighttime viewing is the ultimate. A greenish aura casts what some say is a "mystical, enchanting" spell.

While Jessick was thrilled with the overwhelming reception to his frozen pilgrimage, he remained in relentless pursuit of the crucifix's missing right arm.

His efforts paid off when local photographer Bruce Gathman was sharing stories of the ice homage with another photographer, who turned out to be none other than Ron Tocco . . . from Wyandotte. It has to be more than coincidence that for decades Tocco kept the arm, using it as a paperweight.

The answer to numerous prayers came in February 1997, when both Jessick and Tocco's son, Jay, dived down in the bitter-cold waters of Lake Michigan and ceremoniously reattached the right arm of Jesus.

The winter ice viewings take place in February, weather permitting, and throughout the rest of the year divers can view the crucifix in Little Traverse Bay, just off the pier in Petoskey. For more information call the Petoskey Visitors Bureau at (800) 845-2828 or (231) 348-2755, or visit www.petoskeyarea.com.

Aquanaut Sinks Spirits

The Superior Marine Divers Club invited the late actor Lloyd Bridges to the dedication of the underwater crucifix in 1962. At the time it appeared to be an appropriate gesture since Bridges was starring in the popular TV series *Sea Hunt.*

The actor's response declining the invitation showed that although he may have been hard at work, it apparently wasn't paying off. The Western Union Telegram was sent from West Hollywood, California . . . collect.

★ ★

May the Force Be with You
Putney Corners

A desolate country road in northern Michigan has all the trappings for becoming another Blair County prodigy, already endowed with its own cult following. People from all over the state drive to Putney Road for an experience some call mystical, and others simply refer to as baffling.

There's a small section of the road, bordered by cornfields, that seemingly zaps your car backward uphill without any effort on your part at all. Shaking your head in disbelief, like everyone else, you'll try not once but several times over, certain each subsequent attempt will unlock the mystery. It doesn't.

Common sense says the whole thing is an optical illusion. Folklore says the power comes from Blaine Christian Church at the top of the hill, pulling all the sinners back into its fold. Makes sense. No one has left the area without "feeling" the tug.

Although we came pretty close. Giving it that old college try, several times, my husband swore he felt something; I felt nothing. Then a car leaving the only house in sight stopped to give us the bad news. We were on the wrong side of the street.

For guaranteed success, take these directions and a good compass . . . From northbound Highway 31 in the southern portion of Benzie County, go to Joyfield Road. Turn left onto Joyfield and continue to Putney Road. When you see the church, that's Putney Corners . . . Make a left turn, heading south, and drive down to the bottom of the first hill, a few hundred feet, until you can spot the STOP AHEAD sign in your rearview mirror. Drop into neutral, and you'll soon find yourself motoring skyward in reverse. Two important reminders: Be sure you're on the south side of Putney, off Joyfield, and that there's not another vehicle behind you. If you do get lost, try reaching the Benzie County Chamber of Commerce at (231) 882-5801 or (800) 882-5801, or check them out at www.benzie.org. It's completely free and may be Michigan's best kept secret.

While there's no question the phenomenon is fun, don't you wonder what circumstances provoked someone to discover it in the first place?

To Float, Empty Your Mind . . .
and Other Words by Larry Mawby
Suttons Bay

> A winemaking poet, his claim to fame
> The sign out front says L. Mawby's his name
> Twelve acres of land with a pen in hand
> Become wisdom-laced bubbly, tops in the land*

> *Blanc de Blanc*
> *She's light, she's lively*
> *Blonde and bubbly,*
> *She's not French, but her kiss makes your tongue dance.*

Those are the words of Larry Mawby, who's been inking imaginative, free-flowing verse, "most obscene and unprintable," since he was an English major at Michigan State. For the last quarter century, he's also been whipping up liquid spirits in glass bottles and magnums from his vineyard, crediting Senator Ted Kennedy for the opportunity to combine his two favorite forms of palate pleasing.

When the government initiated its policy requiring warning labels on all alcoholic beverages, Mawby's outrage would have been good competition for Shaquille O'Neal. It compelled him to tag each product with his personal poetic trademark.

Of course the powers-that-be still had to eagle eye every word, and some of those words have raised an eyebrow or two.

> *Mille*
> *Our fine girl swirl is one in a thousand*
> *And a mature-scented-miss*
> *mystery with tongue loving curves.*

* *Not* written by L. Mawby

There were questions on that one, but it passed, as did Turkey Red, Bad Dog, and Tattoo, without one word-smoothing adjustment.

For tastings of any of his interestingly named bubbly, or to receive a copy of his "infrequent newsletter," reach L. Mawby at 4519 South Elm Valley Road; (231) 271-3522; or www.lmawby.com.

Bottle and Fruit: Everlastingly Peared
Suttons Bay

First-time visitors to Black Star Farms agricultural estate are incessantly mesmerized by the Pear and its Spirit, a bottle of 80-proof brandy with a large, ripe, perfectly shaped pear lodged permanently inside. How do you get a seemingly unadulterated piece of fruit to fit through the narrow opening? Partner Don Coe quips it's a Clinton pear and he's "taught it to inhale."

Your eyes cast a glance on acres filled with paradoxical growth, bottles sprouting from branches, convincing you that too much time was spent in the vineyard tasting room. Things aren't always what they first appear to be, and a closer inspection confirms that it's the fruit going through the internal growing pains. Michigan is one of two states in the country (Oregon is the other) where hand-tying bottles to trees is a work of art.

It takes time and some of Mother Nature's blessings to produce the perfect pear, and while the end result is a noble conversation piece, it comes with a price . . . $74.50 a bottle. It's an exemplary Michigan gift, and even high-ranking state officials have been known to ask for a discount, only to be given the same answer as everyone else . . . no. Why should they get a break when at least $43 of that price is the tax imposed by the state? With this in mind, Coe had an enterprising thought—pass a law making it mandatory for every adult residing in Michigan to purchase one pear in a bottle. As of the 2010 census, Michigan recorded 9,883,640 residents. Assuming two-thirds of them are of legal drinking age, creating a potential influx of an estimated 280.5 million tax dollars, headlines everywhere would read,

**A glass womb bottles up its baby pear,
waiting until it gets to drinking age.**

"Michiganians drink their way to state's profitability." Might not be a bad idea after all.

The vineyards here sit on the forty-fifth parallel, sharing that distinction with the Burgundy region of France, the two producing grapes that are indistinguishable from one another. Sample for yourself from an extensive selection, including their unique "ice" wines, at 10844 East Revold Road. An attractive B&B, equestrian center, and creamery round out the estate. For reservations or information call (231) 944-1270 or visit www.blackstarfarms.com.

Driveway Name Gains Worldwide Fame
Traverse City

James and Mildred Bender were sitting at home watching the news one night in February 2006, when across the TV screen flashed footage of the sign at the end of their driveway. Why is their sign newsworthy? Because unbeknownst to them, it had just captured first place in the nation's wackiest street name contest.

An online poll sponsored by www.thecarconnection.com brought in hundreds of nominations of offbeat street names, including the second and third place Divorce Court in Pittston, Pennsylvania, and Farfrompoopen Road in Arkansas. It was a woman from Leelanau County who submitted the grand prize winner—Psycho Path, a name James Bender had come up with on a whim in 2003.

Enter at your own risk.

Overnight fame came to the man who ran the Traverse City Flap Jack restaurant for thirty-five years and his "crazy" street. It seemed as though every major news outlet in the world ran the story. He appeared on the *Today* show. *Reader's Digest* covered it in its May 2006 edition.

The irony is that Psycho Path isn't a street at all. It's Bender's driveway. As he says, he "might have the only named driveway anywhere." After winning the contest, national news departments called the offices at Solon Township where officials told them it wasn't a certified street. The media didn't care. After all, why let facts get in the way of a perfectly good story?

Bender's getting a good chuckle out of the whole thing. Originally he had put up an official-looking green and white road sign, only to have it stolen. The new one is blue and white, so as not to be confused with the county roads.

People drive by all the time to take pictures of the sign. The home at 2025 Highway 72 (about ten miles west of Traverse City) isn't visible from the road, and those who do venture down the long and winding "Psycho Path" driveway have a heck of a time turning around to leave.

The Great Cherry Pie Debate
Traverse City

The Cherry Capital of the world is Traverse City, confirmed by its Cherry Capital Airport and the prodigious cherry crop it produces. Within the city limits sit the remains of the "World's Largest Cherry Pie." Or is it? The giant pie cries have become fightin' words to the city of Charlevoix, keeping the cities forty-five minutes and some 20,000 pounds of cherries apart.

Each city claims to have, at one point in its history, rolled out the biggest edible cherry pie. Each proudly displays physical proof of the pie's existence. Now it's time to present the facts to the jury.

The Charlevoix pie was created in 1976 with 4,950 pounds of tart red cherries and a cumulative weight of 14,000 pounds, including

Ever wonder what a pie pan that can hold 18,350 pounds of cherries looks like? Now you can see for yourself.

top and bottom crust, with a diameter of fourteen feet, four inches. Traverse City's pie, baked on July 25, 1987, by Chef Pierre Bakeries, is authenticated by the *Guinness Book of World Records* to have had a net weight of 28,350 pounds (without a bottom crust), measuring seventeen feet, six inches in diameter.

Today, all that's left of Traverse's pie is the pan, standing in front of the Sara Lee Bakery (formerly Chef Pierre Bakeries). In Charlevoix, their pan stands with one lonesome piece of pie still intact. If the pie was that good in the first place, don't you think someone would have sampled that piece by now?

Check out the evidence for yourself. In Charlevoix, the tin and its fossilized piece can be seen in front of the Fire Department Station #2 at 6591 South US 31. The address for the Traverse City certifiable pie (maybe we're all certifiable for even debating the issue) is 3424 Cass Road on the landscape adjacent to the current Sara Lee facilities. While you're there, quench your appetite for cherry pie from the Sara Lee outlet around the corner. (For the rest of the story and its continuing saga, see the Charlevoix entry.)

I Smooched the Moose

Traverse City

You might be surprised to learn that people drive from hours away to kiss a ninety-year-old moose. But they do. And they've been doing it for years, although no one remembers when the tradition actually began.

Sleder's Family Tavern, believed to be Michigan's oldest continuously operating tavern, opened its doors in 1882. Where once only men sat and drank, today men, women, and children come to enjoy good food and fun.

Everyone hears bells ring when they get their first kiss from Randolph.

★ ★

Part of that fun includes smacking lips with Randolph, a 1,500-pound moose hung on the wall in a traditional kissing mount. Randolph's lovable legend is a mystery, although there have been some theories that provide fodder for folks. Some hypothesize that puckering up started out as a soccer team initiation. Others say the moose was so big, hunters used to kiss him for good luck on their own pursuit. Bartender Andy Swan says, "It's got to be good luck. Either that or they get the flu."

Whatever the reason, his name is no secret. At a moose naming party one night at the tavern, patrons were asked to applaud for the moniker of their choice. Nothing was clicking with the crowd . . . until one drunk looked at the street sign and yelled out, "Randolph." Everyone loved it. And Randolph he became.

Sleder's Family Tavern is found at 717 Randolph Street; (231) 947-9213. For more information visit www.sleders.com.

Milk Her for All She's Worth
Traverse City

An abandoned set of buildings sits in architectural splendor, vestige of an era many residents today would like to forget. It's the site of the former Traverse City State Hospital, the silent word *mental* fitting in there somewhere, home to hundreds of patients from the late 1800s right through the 1970s.

But one occupant lies down above all others to this very day—Traverse Colantha Walker, the greatest lactating cow ever known to hand, buried on the premises where she was known to really put out . . . 200,114.9 pounds of milk and 7,525.8 pounds of butterfat.

The bountiful bovine contributed more than her fair share to the farming operations, considered therapeutic at the time. Packing 2,000 bushels of tomatoes and sixty-five barrels of cabbage was thought to render the same effect as Prozac. Other animals subsidized nutritional needs for poultry and pork, and at one time a huge piggery stood

★ ★

where a junior high school stands today. The local historical society pushed for "Piggery" as the official school name, but that didn't pan out. Instead it became the unimaginatively named West Junior High.

Ms. Walker's monumental tombstone, expressing all her vital statistics, sits at the side of the road, near the barns where she left her mark. A huge banquet was held to commemorate her passing in 1932, where I've heard she was eulogized by guests feasting on royal portions of prime rib.

The cow now has her own festival the second Sunday in June. For more information call (231) 941-1900 or visit www.thevillagetc.com.

Located on the west side of Traverse City, west of US Highway 31 (Division Street), north of Meijer Thrifty Acres. Turn west onto 11th Street (watch for the stone pyramid) and continue straight. The noted grave site is on the dirt road (Red Drive) opposite Building 217.

TRAVERSE COLANTHA WALKER
361604
BORN 4-29-1916
DIED 1-8-1932
WORLD'S CHAMPION COW
MILK 200,114.9 LBS.
FAT 7,525.8 LBS.
NINE LACTATIONS
BRED, OWNED, DEVELOPED
BY TRAVERSE CITY HOSPITAL

A giant tombstone marks the grave of Michigan's foremost dairy queen.

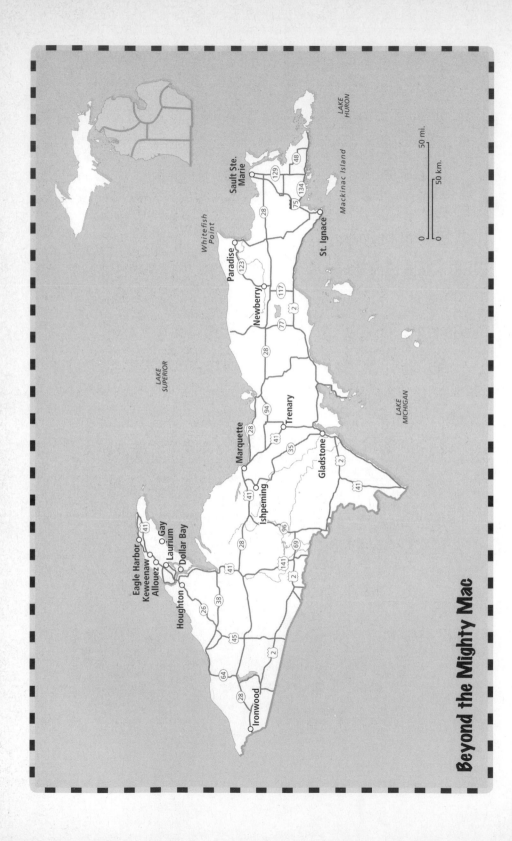

Beyond the Mighty Mac

6

Beyond the Mighty Mac

Admittedly, "Beyond the *Big Mac" has a better ring to it, but if there's one thing you don't want to do, it's getting a Yooper ticked, eh, especially if you're a troll. Translation: You don't want to anger a resident of the Upper Peninsula (Yooper) if you're someone who lives in the Lower Peninsula (troll, as in under the bridge).*

The Mackinac Bridge, the longest suspension bridge in the Western Hemisphere—approaching five miles in length—has been a symbol of unification for Michigan as well as a heck of a good deal for passengers. In 1923, the first year that ferry boats crossed the Straits of Mackinac, 10,351 vehicles were transported to the tune of $2.50 a car. By 1950, 600,000 sets of wheels waited up to twelve hours during deer hunting season and weekends to make that same trip. The delay was permanently eliminated on November 1, 1957, when the "Mighty Mac" opened to traffic. And unlike most fares, this one hasn't gone up much—today a one-way trip is $ $3.50 per crossing. Unless of course it's Labor Day, the one day out of the year when you can walk across for free.

To set the record straight, Mackinac Island is officially a resident of the Upper Peninsula, is always pronounced Mackinaw, even though the French spelling throws most people, and sells so much fudge that daytrippers here are affectionately labeled "fudgies."

Besides the sweet smell of confections, the UP is the home of smoked fishy jerky and pasties, a meat pie popularized by the copper miners. You can always pick out the true Yoopers if they pronounce it correctly on the first try. Pass tee *is the pie, not to be confused with* paste tee *the, um, well, let's not touch that definition. Trust me, there's quite a difference between the two.*

Inspired by the environs, you'll find sites like Eckerman's Bear Butt Inn or billboards promoting Moose Joose Koolwater. And coming from a family of Yoopers myself, I can safely say once a Yoofer, always a Yooper, curiously summed up on one local license plate as: up4ever.

✦ ✦

The Last Place on Earth
Allouez

In Marketing 101, on the first day of class, the first thing you learn is not to name a store "The Last Place on Earth." It might be a great concept to sell condos in the event of a space invasion, but certainly not what you'd want to call an art, antiques, and collectibles shop.

When Tom and Jan Manniko first purchased their store, in 1968, there was, to put it mildly, a little work to do. Even though Tom was a woodworker, his wife, Jan, remembers that when he finished, he said, "I wouldn't do this again if it were the last place on earth." When Jan's friends from Miami asked her about the new venture, she repeated Tom's theme and the name stuck.

With more trees than a woodpecker's fantasy, the Upper Peninsula has a long tradition of woodworking, and the big sellers at the store are Tom's various types of wooden bowls, plates, and spoons. Each piece is made individually by hand to guarantee a uniqueness that is missing in so much of today's craftsmanship.

Tom has plenty of time to work on his wood carving since the store operates only seasonally, which in this area of the Upper Peninsula means "sometime after the thaw to sometime before the first big snow."

Time seems to take on a different perspective in an area that routinely gets 187.4 inches of snow each year. They don't call it Big Snow Country for nothing.

In fact, back in the winter of 1978-79, Keweenaw County got a record 390.4 inches of snow. That's more than thirty-two feet.

While Tom is shoveling, snowblowing, and woodworking, Jan has the time to sort out the antiques and collectibles she sells to the summertime folks on their way up to the uppermost tip of Michigan, Copper Harbor.

By the way, for those of you like me who are knickknack-impaired when it comes to collectibles versus antiques, Jan told me that a collectible is technically something between fifty and a hundred years old, while an antique has to be more than a hundred to qualify. The tough

★ ★

part, according to Jan, is knowing the difference between fifty-year-old collectible junk and hundred-year-old antique junk.

You'll find The Last Place on Earth at 59621 US Highway 41. They're closed during the winter. When the weather's warm, they're open seven days a week. Call (906) 337-1014.

More Than a Floor Store
Dollar Bay

They produce a product that is probably used by the most elite group of millionaires in the world. The Horner Flooring Company makes what NBA superstars step onto every night of the season as well as countless practice sessions. Horner floors at high schools and colleges are the "floor of dreams" for thousands of NBA wannabes worldwide.

Back in 1891, when William S. Horner converted an existing pine planing mill to hardwood floor manufacturing, he probably didn't think the company would become the oldest name in hardwood flooring, but by the time he moved the facility from the Lower Peninsula to the Upper in 1914 it was on its way to becoming the world's largest producer of hardwood flooring. Today, at its 60,000-square-foot facility in Dollar Bay, Michigan, Horner makes the Pro-King portable basketball floor that has been used in the NBA all-star games and the NCAA championship play-offs.

If the concept of a portable basketball floor seems strange, you just have to look at the economics of modern arenas. The jump ball at the start of an NBA game tonight might be center stage for a concert by Britney Spears tomorrow night, center ice for a college hockey game on the weekend, and the center ring for the Flying Fannuti Family in a circus the day after that.

Believe it or not, the Pro-King basketball floor used at the Palace of Auburn Hills, home of the Detroit Pistons, Detroit Vipers of the IHL, and more events than even Donald Trump could attend, can be installed by the experienced crew there in only six to eight man-hours. The secret is the way the 203 four-by-eight-foot panels and fourteen four-by-four-foot panels are guided into position and fastened with a hidden sliding lock. It's all part of a patented system that is part of the floor panel itself so it can't be mislaid or damaged. The subflooring allows for changes in humidity for a tight-fitting, level playing surface that means less chance of leg or ankle injuries. What good is a multimillion-dollar basketball shoe endorsement deal if one of your multimillion-dollar feet is in a cast?

But don't take my word for it. Ask the Pistons, Nuggets, Jazz, Kings, Celtics, and Trailblazers. The players might not know where the floors are from, but I'll bet they'd be able to identify with any place named Dollar Bay.

The Horner Flooring Company is on 23400 Hellman Drive. Call (906) 482-1180 or visit www.hornerflooring.com.

A Slice of Heaven with Jam On It
Eagle Harbor

A berry and a prayer are the two things responsible for creating a thriving business in the sparsely populated Keweenaw Peninsula.

It all began in 1983, when two young men who had just graduated from the University of Michigan were searching for somewhere to "embrace the struggle of life in a hard place." They felt a calling to the coldest and snowiest place in all of Michigan, where they purchased a three-acre parcel of land with five small buildings, no insulation, and running water only half the year.

Soon after affiliating with the Byzantine Church the next spring, the two new monks stumbled upon the thimbleberry, a fragile wild fruit, similar to a jumbo raspberry and a cousin to the blackberry. Conquering both bears and poison ivy, Fathers Nicholas and Basil passionately picked the delicate berry, transforming it into a uniquely delicious jam.

Good news spreads fast. Good food spreads even quicker and it wasn't long before customers were pouring in. Along with that came a few more monks, eager to put their time and talents to good use. Their thimbleberry jam had planted the seed for their success.

Fr. Basil puts his gentle touch on the baked goods
that "jam" his quaint store with customers.
ANDY DUBILL

On Memorial Day weekend in 1990, the Jampot officially opened,
containing a completely renovated kitchen. Four years later came the
parking lot, with space for tour buses and mobile homes. And 1996
brought the warehouse, a workshop, and snow removal equipment
(finally).

Their menu now includes an expanding assortment of jams, breads,
chocolate truffles, and cakes. A real winner is their Abbey Cake, filled
with raisins and pecans, all "liberally laced with Jack Daniel's."

After constant prayers and the generosity of donors, the
monks now have their own church, too. The onion-domed Holy

Transfiguration sits proudly on the shore of Lake Superior surrounded by stunning gardens, lovingly dosed with wildflowers.

Cold temperatures aside, boundless beauty survives here all four seasons. Clearly, divine intervention allowed humans to see what the thimbleberries knew all along: This place really is Heaven on Earth.

The Jampot can be found at the Holy Transfiguration Skete, 6559 State Highway M26, Eagle Harbor. It's open 10:00 a.m. to 5:00 p.m., Monday through Saturday, May to mid-October. There's no phone, but there is a website: www.societystjohn.com. Mail orders are filled year-round.

The Gay Bar
Gay

No it isn't. Since the entire population of Gay, Michigan, is only thirty-six people, Bruce and Chris Fountain couldn't afford to cater to any specific group when they bought the Gay Bar after moving to this burg on the shores of Lake Superior.

The town itself is named for Joseph R. Gay, a mining superinten-dent who christened it in 1936. Back then the saloon was just a place for miners to stop and quench their thirst after a day in the pits.

Although there are gay bars all over the country, there is only one "the Gay Bar." It's a typical Upper Peninsula bar. When you walk in, don't expect to see Richard Simmons impersonators doing a dinner theater version of *Funny Girl.* You're more likely to hear the latest on how the Green Bay Packers are doing. The Upper Peninsula is big-time Packer country, so if you're a Lions fan, prepare to get grief. Of course if you're a Lions fan, you're used to it.

As for entertainment, Chris says, "We entertain ourselves." Since the bar is horseshoe-shaped, just about any remark triggers a discussion. Despite the town's population, during snowmobile season (which is probably about nine months long) it's not uncommon to see seventy or eighty "sleds" (as the folks around here call them) in the parking lot. In the wintertime the snowmobile trails are used as much as the roads.

The spring thaw brings the annual Gay volleyball tournament, and the Fourth of July Gay Parade draws more than 1,500 people.

In the fall is the Annual Big Buck Ball contest, during which deer hunters who didn't want to lug in antlers were allowed to compete in a much less cumbersome fashion. The 6¾-ounce winning pair was toasted all around and, we suppose, mourned by the does in the area.

The Gay Bar is now on the Internet, so their big sellers are available worldwide. They sell assorted hats, lighters, can coolers, as well as T-shirts that feature cartoons appropriate for the bar's specialty: a foot-long hot dog.

It's not that Chris and Bruce are greedy. If they were, they would have decided long ago to start charging for pictures that every tourist seems to want to take in front of their place at the GAY BAR sign. Look for the Gay Bar at 925 Lake Street. The phone number is (906) 296-0951; the website is www.thegaybar.com.

A Tisket, A Casket for Lizards, Snakes, and Squirrels
Gladstone

Finding good entertainment in the Upper Peninsula must be harder than anyone expected. And just when you thought you'd heard all the options, along comes someone inviting you to accompany him on a tour of the Hoegh Pet Casket Factory, guaranteed to be the only one like it in the universe.

The Hoegh family has been serving the needs of pet lovers since 1966 with their exclusive line of pink and blue caskets. As their literature enticingly expresses, this is a golden opportunity to "view the manufacture of pet caskets and tour a model pet cemetery." Oh, boy.

Not nearly as dreadful as you might imagine, one of the company's nine employees takes you through the cookie-cutter process of transforming a flat sheet of plastic into a vacuum-molded casket. Due to the limitations of the molds, no special orders are accepted, although choices go far beyond a one-size-fits-all. Dimensions are standardized starting at ten-by-four inches to accommodate itty-bitty gerbils or

You won't find any dog bones in this cemetery. The rows of headstones are only "demos" sitting behind the Hoegh Pet Casket Factory.
J. HOEGH

fish, up to the fifty-two-inch jumbo deluxe, large enough to fit a lion, which on an infrequent basis has been done.

The tours are designed to acquaint people with the concept of a proper burial for any animal that's been near and dear to their heart, not just the traditional household cats and dogs, allowing you, without guilt, to "think outside of the box." The company acknowledges that their caskets have been the final resting home for ferrets, lizards, a boa constrictor, squirrels, skunks, a monkey, and a pet chicken.

Caskets are shipped to seven hundred locations, some as far away as Puerto Rico and Africa, to the tune of more than 35,000 a year, not including the 7,500 cremation urns, evidence that this is not a dying business. (I know, it's a groaner.)

While it's impossible to keep track of where every casket ends up, a local customer placed a questionable order for a forty-incher for a pet Chihuahua. When confronted regarding the unusual sizing request, she responded, "We wanted extra space so there'll be plenty of room to run around."

Hoegh Pet Casket Factory and Model Cemetery is located at 317 Delta Avenue and is open for tours Monday through Friday. Call (906) 428-2151 or log on to www.hoeghpetcaskets.com.

Carnival—Snow Different than Rio
Houghton

What's a college kid to do in the middle of January watching more than two hundred inches of snow fall outside the dormitory window? Celebrate with a bone-chilling cry—"It's Carnival Time!"

Being ever so resourceful when it comes to finding a purpose to party, the Blue Key National Honor Fraternity devised the idea of a winter carnival in 1934 at Michigan Technological University, now home to more than 7,000 students.

Like the rhythmic sounds filling the streets of Rio during Carnival, the snowdrifts of Houghton are aflutter with echoes of sizzling-hot irons, buzzing saws, whirling machetes, and a host of other hand tools crafting out chunks of white stuff. Sprinkle in some Jell-O or powdered paint with twenty-eight hours of uninterrupted "engineering home-work" and the result is . . . the renowned snow sculptures.

The popularity of this time-honored tradition has grown so that in 2002 school officials instituted a round-the-clock statue cam over the Internet to satisfy the demand from friends and alumni worldwide to watch the snow transform before their eyes, too. An astounding

★ ★

**An all-nighter for students at Michigan Tech
turns out chilling artistic beauty.**
UPPER PENINSULA TRAVEL & RECREATION ASSOCIATION

220,000 people logged on, making everyone, except the systems director, extremely happy.

The whole carnival scene stretches out for a month, even though the snow stays quite a bit longer, with human "dogsled" racing and broomball among the special events. You haven't lived until you've been exposed to broomball. Students cut off the sweeper's bristles halfway up, wrap them in duct tape, then head to the hockey rink in

★ ★

their tennis shoes to whisk a soccer ball through the goalie's box. Do not try this at home . . . leave it for the professionals at Michigan Tech.

The oldest event is choosing the festival's queen, a decision not to be taken lightly. During the selection of the 1939 Winter Carnival Queen, the deciding vote was cast by none other than Mr. White Christmas himself, Bing Crosby. Each year the queen is appropriately coronated with a copper crown, keeping alive the historical significance of the copper mines here.

If you have any questions, you'll get a warm reception from the university's PR staff at (906) 487-2354. Statue cam only operates during Carnival, but the website is accessible year-round at www.mtu.edu/carnival.

Triple Record-breaking Winter

Michigan Tech's 2006 Winter Carnival was an avalanche when it came to breaking *Guinness* world records.

First, more than one hundred students, including twenty weightlifters, rolled a snowball with a diameter of 6.77 feet inside the school's football stadium. The largest snowball previously recorded was five feet four inches in diameter. Second, 3,762 people battled it out using cold, packed ammunition to earn the title of the world's largest snowball fight. Then they all dropped to the ground, picked up a few more friends, and started flapping their wings, earning 3,780 students the title of largest single-venue snow angel event in history and making Mom and Dad very proud their education dollars are being well spent.

Hiawatha Towers Over Town
Ironwood

One household in Ironwood peers out its front window every day, casting an eye on the world's tallest Indian's backside. Gee, how lucky can you get?

Hiawatha was especially designed for the people of Ironwood in 1964 to attract more attention to the area where the now caved-in iron ore mines once stood, at the end of Burma Street. Mission accomplished. Perched high above the city, everybody enjoys some side of him as he hovers over them. Yet the price for his watchful eye was not cheap. Even back then, his fiffy-two-foot-high fiberglass body was constructed to the tune of $10,000.

Traveling through the night so his arrival would be a surprise, the surprise wound up being his disappearance. Hiawatha had been hijacked. Pandemonium broke out, and the national press corps was called in to help pinpoint his whereabouts. Less than twenty-four hours later he was found, safe and sound, with no admission of guilt.

His own special "Erection Ceremony"—the exact words the Hiawatha Committee chose for his official homecoming—went without a hitch as he was anchored into fifty-five yards of concrete with 5,000 pounds of steel reinforcement while the "Saddleites" circled around on horseback. With the "carnival-like" atmosphere, peddlers were in their glory, hawking special shipments of Hiawatha earthenware replicas from Japan to commemorate the occasion.

Souvenir Hiawatha sweatshirts, buttons, notecards, ornaments, and magnets are currently available through the Chamber of Commerce. To make a purchase or just to find out more about this friendly Indian with the twenty-six-foot-long peace gesture, call (906) 932-1122 or visit www.ironwoodmi.org.

★ ★

Stormy Kromer . . . The Cap with the Flap
Ironwood

"It's just common sense—when you can see your breath outside, you put on a hat. When you can snap off your breath and use it to stir your coffee, some additional wardrobe enhancements might be in order."

—Stormy Kromer Co.

Thank Michigan for saving the ultimate wardrobe enhancement . . . the Stormy Kromer. Most people in the state will quickly identify it as a six-panel wool cap with distinctive pull-down earflaps that would make anyone look like a sexy geek (never again will you see those last two words in the same sentence).

A little history first. George "Stormy" Kromer was a semi-professional baseball player who once hit eighteen foul balls before striking out with the bases loaded. After hanging up his cleats, he became a locomotive engineer. In 1905 his frustration with the mid-western winds ripping off his railroad hat led his wife, Ida, to creatively solve the problem. She sewed earflaps onto one of Stormy's old base-ball caps, thus making the new headgear "unflappable"—no matter how high the winds. A new fad was born, and in 1919 the Kromers opened a manufacturing plant in Milwaukee.

But the fickle winds of fashion changed direction, and after almost a century the Stormy was facing extinction. Stepping up to the plate, Ironwood's Bob Jacquart hit a home run by purchasing the operation and moving it to the Upper Peninsula.

Today more than twenty of the 160 people working in the Jacquart textile plant dedicate their skills to hand sewing every one of the 43,000 Stormy Kromers that are sold worldwide each year. The company aims to conquer the head-warming industry; encouraging even the most resistant with clever motivational slogans such as "A frosty head only looks good on beer" and "A great cap makes up for a bad barber."

The Stormy Kromer definitely isn't your grandfather's hat anymore. Fifty US soldiers in Iraq received them for Christmas in 2005. Also that

The Michigan-made Stormy Kromer cap has been transforming guys like this into "chick magnets" since 1903.

COURTESY STORMY KROMER MERCANTILE

year, all thirteen members of the Houghton Gremlins girl's basketball team received a personalized Stormy Kromer to commemorate their state championship title, adding validity to the company's claim that "Warm brains are happy brains." Just ask President Barack Obama who was awarded own Kromer cap when speaking in Marquette on February 20, 2011.

The caps come with a lifetime guarantee, so if one ever wears out, they'll replace it for free. You can watch your own Stormy Kromer being made on one of the public factory tours, offered weekdays at 1:30 p.m. The plant is located at 1238 Wall Street in Ironwood. Phone (888) 455-2253 or view the entire collection at www.stormykromer .com.

★ ★

Da Yooper Tourist Trap

Ishpeming

Yooper (*You-per*, n.): A person from the Upper Peninsula of Michigan.

If there's ever an award for truth in advertising, Da Yooper Tourist Trap wins hands-down. When one of the "hooks" on a billboard to attract customers is free bathrooms, you don't walk in with high expectations. But surprisingly, those expectations are surpassed.

The first thing you notice when you walk through the corridor into the building is a Yooper museum of sorts. There you can see artifacts of life in the Big Snow Country: what they wore, what they hunted, the type of instruments they played to amuse themselves.

Amusement is the key word with the Tourist Trap. It was founded by Jim DeCaire and Lynn Coffey of the band Da Yoopers: a group of Upper Peninsula musicians who have made a real name for themselves singing and fooling around on stages all over Michigan. The band can best be described as a kind of Spike Jones meets Monty Python and moves to the Upper Peninsula. Some of their big hits include "The Second Week of Deer Camp," "Grandpa Got Run Over by a Beer Truck," "Who Goosed the Moose?" and the tender love ballad "Super Dooper Yooper Love Machine." Their musical style includes everything but good taste. That's not to say it's not entertaining, just not always tasteful.

The marketing job that this store does for the band makes Kim Kardashian look publicity-shy. In addition to selling their five CDs and eight cassettes, the store sells an assortment of gag products that makes them money off the trolls (people who live in the Lower Peninsula, under the Mackinaw Bridge).

After pointing out that the Upper Peninsula has a large Finnish population that "likes to poke fun at ourselves," salesperson Einona Heikkila told me I could purchase a "Yooper calculator," which is a small wood cutout of feet with ten toes ($1.99). The "Yooper word processor" is a pencil stub, yours for only $1.50; the "Yooper night-light" is a small tree branch with a candle in it ($3.99); and if you really want to impress your fellow board members at the next big meeting, walk in carrying a "Yooper briefcase": a pair of jockey shorts with handles ($5.99).

You can't miss Da Yooper Tourist Trap: just look for a truck with a giant shotgun mounted on top. It's found at 490 North Steel Street. Contact (800) 628-9978 or www.dayoopers.com. Hours vary.

Snow Way to Go But Up
Keweenaw

There's no business like snow business, at least in northern Michigan. And keeping track of it has become a glamorous full-time job for the Keweenaw Snow Thermometer, which performs the difficult task of pointing with the grace and style of Vanna White.

The thirty-two-foot-high thermometer has been busy indicating annual snow depths since the 1950s. The tall, painted, heavy-duty pole has had its end stuck in the ground 24/7 year-round, measuring how much of the white stuff has fallen while visitors "ooh" and "ahh" over the results.

Originally a pulley would raise the bar on a daily basis. But even the pulley grew tired of the cold, often freezing in mid-action. After a couple of years, a replacement bar was installed, with the much easier task of moving only once a year at the end of the snow season, which has been known to go as late as May. In 2007, the gauge received a face-lift of sorts, with new paint—though still with a white base with a red marker—and all new wooden panels.

A large plaque sits alongside the thermometer stating that the record for new snowfall here occurred during the winter of 1978-79, tabulating a seasonal total of 390.4 inches. It continues, "This could be a new record set in the USA for the entire area east of the Rockies." In case you're interested, December was the snowiest month, chalking up 116.4 inches, followed close behind by January with 111.4 inches.

There's almost a feeling of reverence to snow in these parts. The Keweenaw Road Commission is the keeper of the thermometer and

Snow kidding . . . this thermometer only rises in the cold.
ANDY DUBILL

thankfully admits, "If we weren't up to our eyeballs in snow, we wouldn't have a job."

The Keweenaw Snow Thermometer isn't hard to spot, positioned statuesquely on US Highway 41 at the top of Cliff Hill, just north of Mohawk. Contact the Keweenaw Road Commission at (906) 337-1610.

(Snow thermometer junkies can get their fix with another one in Mancelona in the Lower Peninsula. The twenty-five-footer stands near the railroad track at the corner of US 131 and State Streets.)

Score Big for the Gipper

Laurium

When Ronald Reagan was campaigning for president, the nation united with its rallying cry "Win one for the Gipper"—a phrase he'd immortalized with his portrayal of George Gipp in the 1940 movie *Knute Rockne—All American*. Most of those chanting were unaware Gipp, who originally uttered those words, was a born and bred Yooper with unbelievable athletic prowess.

As a University of Notre Dame freshman in 1916, Gipp's first experience in organized football found him drop-kicking a sixty-two-yard field goal. During his tenure in South Bend, he racked up a win–loss record of 27–2 with three ties, personally executing eighty-three touchdowns.

Overall he handled the pigskin far better than he handled books, both overshadowed by his love of wine, women, and song, and in 1919 administrators said adios, voting on his expulsion. A near rebellion broke out on campus, forcing officials to reverse their decision, and Gipp was back tossing the ball, but not for long. A serious throat infection soon found him sidelined.

His condition worsened, and it was at his bedside that Coach Rockne broke the headlining news of his selection as Notre Dame's first all-American. To that Gipp responded, "Sometime, Rock, when the team's up against it, when things are wrong, when the breaks

✦ ✦

are beating the boys, tell them to go in there with all they've got and win one for the Gipper. I don't know where I'll be then, but I'll know about it and I'll be happy."

On December 20, 1920, at age twenty-five, George Gipp passed away; his body is buried in Lakeview Cemetery near Calumet.

The Kewanee National Historical Park sponsors walking tours that will escort you to the front door of his birthplace at 432 Hecla Street. A George Gipp monument, fully restored in 1995, sits in the park at the corner of Lake Linden Avenue and Tamarack Street where brick pavers and a flower bed outline the shape of footballs. The folks at the Laurium Chamber are most helpful. Call (906) 337-1600.

Livery Licenses Stable Drivers
Mackinac Island

Parents on Mackinac Island are luckier than most. They don't have to listen to the desperate pleadings for a new car when their children turn sixteen. That's because there are no motorized vehicles of any kind on the island, with the exception of an ambulance, one police car, and two fire trucks. The ban on four wheels officially began as a restriction, permitting them only on tiny French Lane, exclusively during daylight hours so as not to frighten the horses at night. But with the island supported 90 percent by tourism, it was inevitable that charm would prevail. By 1900 tires were out, hooves were in.

And so it is that most youngsters learn to ride a horse before any-thing else. Rather than the acquisition of a driver's license equating to a national holiday, the monumental stepping-stone is birthday number twelve, with the grand prize a license to operate the preferred winter mode of transportation . . . the snowmobile, a privilege granted here two years earlier than anywhere else in the state.

With a once-a-week dentist and no resident barber, it does become necessary to make the occasional trip to the mainland, so eventually each of the eighty students will need to experience the feel of the open road as seen from behind a steering wheel. Thanks to modern

technology, driver's education is accomplished via interactive comput-
ers. When the big day does come to head over to St. Ignace for some
on-the-road experience, it's been said that when pulling up to their
first stoplight, rather than putting on the brakes they simply call out
"Whoa" to the Buick.

And in case you're wondering if anyone on the island has suc-
cumbed to the urge to put the pedal to the metal, the answer is a
resounding yes. Longtime resident Mr. Telifson managed to smuggle in
two touring cars from the early 1900s. When the governor caught him
tooling around under the moonlight in 1948, he claimed the engine
was being used only to pump water out of the lake. Oh, thank heaven
for automatic sprinklers.

No motors on Mackinac Island—horsepower is the rule not to be
broken. The Grand Hotel obliges by transporting its golfers between
the lower and upper nine via the country's only horse-drawn golf cart.

What Ripley Believed, Guinness Did Not

Mackinac Island

There's something about a charming wooden porch that's a guaranteed invitation, whether it's for eats, drinks, or on a rainy day to
provide a cover for a spirited game of tennis. At The Grand Hotel, the
world's longest columned porch sits majestically overlooking the Straits
of Mackinac and, in times of need, has substituted as a home for lobs
and volleys. It's certainly big enough, although its exact size has been
the source of scrutiny and debate.

In 1936 times were tough, competition for tourism dollars was stiff,
and the owner of The Grand, W. Stewart Woodfill—it remains in his
family to this day—became a marketing genius almost overnight. With
an advertising budget of zero, he invented the claim that the hotel's
expansive porch spanned a full 880 feet. For publicity, Robert L. Ripley
was contacted, and believe it or not, he fell for the misnomer, spread-
ing the word in his once heralded column. The very next year a line of
people four miles long waited to sashay across its famed frame.

Hundreds of rockers, seven tons of potting
soil, 260 planting boxes, and 2,500 geraniums
on The Grand Hotel's famous porch.

The record stood for years—forty-six to be exact—until the *Guinness Book of World Records* asked for documentation. Appearing in the fall of 1981 with their own set of surveyors, the measurements revealed the porch was . . . 625 feet. Whoops!

With the latest expansion, the hotel's promenade, accurately computed, fills up 660 feet, although many island tour guides have been overheard continuing to insist it's still 880. Their explanation for the difference? In summer the wood expands, and by the time Guinness arrived, the cool weather had caused a contraction of more than 20 percent.

The popularity of the porch, with its trademark geraniums, has grown so that there's now a charge for non-hotel-guests—$10 a stroll, which can be applied as credit toward breakfast or the Grand Buffet Luncheon. With 1,000 guests a day paying the extra tariff, it's unlikely The Grand Hotel will ever have to resort to fabricated forms of advertising again.

Street addresses are nonexistent on the island. For reservations, call (800) 334-7263—that's (800) 33-GRAND—or visit www.grandhotel .com.

Picasso of Recycling Says, "Welcome to My Junkyard"
Marquette

What do you do when you don't watch TV and your wife tells you to find a new hobby somewhere outside of a bar? If you're Tom Lakenen, you recycle heaps of junk into masterful works of art.

As he cultivated a phenomenal talent, his collection of artistic pieces overwhelmed his front yard, a no-no with township officials. So in 2003, he mortgaged his house "for another 100 years" and bought thirty-seven acres of land, about eight miles from his home, to establish a sculpture park.

Open 24/7 365 days a year to the public (except for Chocolay Township officials, who gave Tom such a hard time—there's a NO TRESPASSING sign for them). You can either walk, drive, or snowmobile through an awesome collection of more than eighty gargantuan metal sculptures, all made from some form of scrap metal. Check out the alligator he's made of rebar from reinforced concrete. A trio of bright yellow sunflowers started out life as sprockets from a bulldozer.

Lakenen doesn't have to pay for his materials, except the paint. Originally he'd bring fellow construction workers a case of beer, saying "It's amazing what they'll give you after that." Word spread fast and neighbors were soon dropping off goods on his doorstep. It was someone's discarded bathtub that prompted him to turn it into a leering old man with a smile on his face and a pin bearing the word *Viagra*.

The Whole Poop, Nothing but the Poop

"Take this job and shovel it." Those are words from Gerry Horn, who was Mackinac Island's chief pooper scooper for thirty-eight years. His job, twelve hours a day, six days a week, was to go around with a wheelbarrow and broom and clean up what the horses left off.

Okay, so the work stinks, but somebody has to do it. With five hundred horses on the island, providing the only means of transportation outside of your own two legs, there's a lot of . . . stuff to pick up. The animals don't wear diapers. Putting in seven-hour shifts, the irritation would be too hard on them. Besides, with a constant breeze in the air, passengers would be the ones experiencing a fragrance more like Chanel No. 2.

★ ★

Lakenen has a great sense of humor as well as an edgy sense of politics. His sculpture of an indignant pink pig stands below a sign GENUINE
NORTH AMERICAN CORPORATE GREED PIG. The finishing touch was put on the
pig's back, where Lakenen tattooed the label *Enron*.

A guest book reveals visitors from practically every one of the United
States, plus Mexico, Germany, Finland, Japan, and Israel. Surprisingly the
busiest time of the year is winter, when as many as 250 snowmobilers a
day visit as Lakenen personally greets them with a warm cup of coffee
and snacks. He even builds a fire inside the dragon statue so it looks like
there's smoke coming out his nose.

**Sanitation is a peak priority. Each night the streets are completely
flushed, and during the day, the shovelers are always on the lookout
for business.**

**But the summer of '02 it wasn't business as usual. A horse-drawn
street sweeper was brought in—talk about multiplying your product—and Gerry Horn had to hang up his broom. His eternally optimis-
tic attitude would have made him the ideal candidate for *Survivor*,
quipping, "I may have been voted off the island, but I ain't leaving."**

**So somebody else will be busy "walking a mile for a pile," and
Horn says he'll no longer have to "break my back for a good stack."
However, the story has a happy ending for this hardworking gentle-
man. The king of one-liners has been reassigned, remaining thankful
for continuing employment. After all, "it may have been horse poop
to you, but it's bread and butter to me."**

In the summer, he has two ponds stocked with blue gill and perch so children can enjoy fishing there.

When will he stop propagating his art? "When I run out of junk."

Lakenenland sits at 2800 East M-28, fifteen miles east of Marquette, or in the middle of Snowmobile Trail 417; www.lakenenland .com. Free admission, although the sign at the front says DONATIONS ACCEPTED, THOUGH NOT EXPECTED.

The artist thinks this could be a "Wisconsin Hodag," built from parts found in a South Marquette rail yard; its tongue is a broken shovel.
ANDY DUBILL

TV's Longest Running Talk Show Host

When it comes to setting records for longevity as a TV talk show host, forget about Oprah. She doesn't even come close to Carl Pellonpa. He's been the star of FINLAND CALLING (SUOMI KUTSUU) on Marquette's WLUC-TV 6 since March 25, 1962. Starting out first as a half-hour program, by the end of April it was extended to a full hour, where it's been ever since.

Camera crews have come and gone through the years, but one thing remains the same: None of them have ever understood a word of what Pellonpa is saying, since his entire show is spoken in Finnish.

Wahlstrom's Restaurant
Marquette

It looks like any other family restaurant when you're driving along US Highway 41 South just outside of Marquette in the Upper Peninsula. And to most of the regulars, that's exactly what Wahlstrom's is.

Customers around here are used to seeing sweet rolls the size of manhole covers and ordering six kinds of hash-brown potatoes that can include every conceivable topping with the exception of hot fudge. Their standard meat eaters' omelet comes with four eggs, bacon, sausage, ham, cheese, and hash browns inside . . . and a side of pancakes.

When founder Roy Wahlstrom got back to Michigan from the service—he was in the first wave on Utah Beach on D-Day—he got a job as the guard at the prison in Marquette. Knowing that his fellow

★ ★

servicemen were used to getting great prices at the military post exchange stores, he opened a coffee shop and named it The PX.

When Wahlstrom noticed that tourists and salesmen were coming to the area and needed a place to stay, he decided to build a motel. While working full time at the prison, he and a carpenter buddy started cutting down trees, clearing the land, and milling the lumber. Before long they had hand-built the first nine motel units and a cafe.

Both prospered, and Wahlstrom decided that a restaurant was the next logical step. So in 1960 he built what is now Wahlstrom's.

Wahlstrom referred to himself as a busy boy—working up to twenty-three hours a day sometimes. He couldn't have been that busy, though; he still had time for eight kids.

The kids seem to have the same kind of energy level as dear old dad. The eldest, Steve, runs the catering business and is a nonstop promotion machine. The youngest, Tom, is a talented chef.

If you're wondering how talented a chef has to be to make six different kinds of hash-brown potatoes, that's where the catering comes in. Want a sit-down dinner for 1,200? Call Wahlstrom's. Want an entire cow cooked on a spit as a birthday surprise? No problem. Wahlstrom's catering is known for being able to handle everything from a pig roast on the shores of Lake Superior where the supplies have to be brought in by boat, to $100-per-plate dinners served on fine china. Who says you can't be all things to all people?

Look for the restaurant at 5045 US Highway 41 South; (906) 249-1453. Open seven days a week, except on holidays.

Papa Bear's House Fits Just Right
Newberry

A typical evening's entertainment in the Upper Peninsula for many years was heading to the garbage dump to watch the bears. With those all closed, the only place you're guaranteed to see bears in northern Michigan anymore is at "Oswald's Dump." Those are Dean Oswald's words, not mine.

Dean Oswald and The Three Bears—at five months old. It's
hard to believe they started life the size of a mouse.

He and his wife, Jewel, are the papa and mama of an eighty-acre
ranch, the largest ranch in the United States dedicated exclusively to
raising bears. Not the most likely career change for someone who
spent nineteen and a half years as a Bay City firefighter and a brief
stint as a professional boxer, yet knew since the 1950s that this was
his heart's true calling.

In 1984 he acquired a license (which you can no longer do in Michigan) and purchased his first bear—appropriately named "Bear"—from
a federal breeder in Wisconsin. Along came another one and another
one . . . and at last count his family consisted of twenty-five black

bears, most trained to come when called, hopefully not too fast since they can run up to 40 mph. Such tender, loving care is administered here that the Michigan Department of Natural Resources sends ailing bears to the Oswalds for a little R&R (that's "recovery and rehabilitation"). All have done so well they've become permanent residents.

A few questions are probably crossing your mind right about now. The answer to the first one is yes. Dean has been bitten, only once, by Tyson, a 1,000-pounder, who died of a heart attack in July 2000. Question number two gets a no: Jewel doesn't cook all fifty-five gallons of food the clan requires each day. Local restaurants contribute their scraps to help out. The response to number three is sometimes. With the bears in hibernation from late October until the third week in March, the Oswalds are able to have some time away from their "beary" busy schedule of responsibilities.

When cubs are small enough, you can have your photo taken holding one of them.

Oswald's Bear Ranch is open every day from the Friday of Memorial Day weekend through September 30. There's a $15 fee per carload, or $10 for individuals; you can either walk around all of the ten- to fifteen-acre habitats or take the tram. The address is 13814 County Road 407 (H37). From Newberry head north for four miles on Highway 123 to Deer Park Road. Turn left and travel another four miles. The bear signs will guide you the rest of the way. Call (906) 293-3147 or visit www.oswaldsbearranch.com.

Follow the Bouncing Berry

Paradise

There's strong evidence that cranberries can either cure or prevent urinary tract infections. If that's true, then the House family, which has been farming them for more than 126 years, must have the healthiest bladders in the world.

Land purchased in 1876 became the Centennial Cranberry Farm, named for our country's hundredth birthday, and has been growing every since, so much that now eighty-five tons of the tart, scarlet gems are harvested each year, most of them shipped out of state and processed into Wal-Mart's private-label juice.

Loren House is the third generation of Houses to till the land of the state's oldest and (until 1993) only cranberry farm, with family members involved in all aspects of the business. His wife, Sharon, oversees the gift shop, situated in the former Whitefish Point Post Office where Sarah House was postmistress from 1907 to 1916, and in her spare time whips up batches of super-delicious cranberry butter.

Nobody feels "bogged" down, though, because once the vines are in place, they hardly ever need replanting. Recently "native" vines more than a hundred years old were uncovered in a brushy area, still reproducing every three years.

Harvesttime is the busiest, usually occurring mid-October, with the majority of the work done mechanically. All berries are obliged to pass the bounce test—the good ones bounce up, the rotten ones fall to the ground. Kinda reminds me of the pencil test when girls go for their first bra fitting: If the pencil stays, you're ready . . . if it falls to the ground, come back in a few months.

The Centennial Cranberry Farm, on 30957 West Wild Cat Road, offers self-guided tours every day, noon to 5:00 p.m. from Memorial Day weekend through October. There's an admission fee per carload; fresh-picked cranberries are available during the harvest, which is usually mid-October. Call (906) 492-3314 or (877) 333-1822, or visit www .centennialcranberry.com.

Vertically Challenged Redefined
St. Ignace

How many times have you come home from a hard day at work and felt like climbing the walls? When Dan McCarthy's on the job, he's walking up walls every day and watching water flow uphill and balancing chairs on two legs. A magician? Nope. As owner and chief tour guide at the Mystery Spot, he's just doing what comes naturally.

**Dan McCarthy (left) demonstrates a vertically
upright position at his legendary Mystery Spot.**

More than two million visitors have stopped by since he opened to
the public in 1955, but perhaps just as many—like McCarthy's own
parents, who decades ago said they "wouldn't stop at that tourist
trap"—have driven by still wondering about the puzzling site.

With an inquisitive mind on the quest for the truth, my car came to a
halt. Within minutes I found myself walking up a short path, leading to
a lopsided shanty where immediately my body felt the mysterious pull.
No joke . . . a light-headed queasiness akin to motion sickness set in,
which it does for 70 percent of visitors. Clutching the handrails, I was
treated to half an hour of mind-boggling, hands-on demonstrations that

kept me both scratching my head and laughing hysterically. Who would believe you could be three inches taller instantly? Or that a ten-pound pendulum would swing undeniably more uphill? Witnessed with my own eyes, the impossible becomes possible. Questioned whether these are optical illusions, McCarthy testifies that the Mystery Spot merely accentuates what nature has already provided.

The story goes that in 1953 surveyors from California were attempting to level their tripod with a plumb-bob—which was being incessantly drawn to the east. They soon discovered the trouble with their equipment existed only in a plot of land some three hundred feet in diameter. Which is precisely what you feel when you're inside the enigmatic zone . . . that tenacious tug to the east, as if you were magnetized. Once outside the area, their apparatus worked perfectly, and you'll be back to feeling normal.

After more than twenty years in the seasonal business, McCarthy says life just doesn't get any better. Named by *Ski Magazine* in 1990 as "ski bum of the year," during the winter he heads to Colorado where he hits the slopes for 120 straight days . . . er, make that 116. The last four he goes golfing.

There's more to do here—miniature golf, a maze, and zip lines will perhaps take your mind off the mysteries you witnessed.

The Mystery Spot is open "rain or shine" from mid-April through the end of October; hours vary. Call (906) 643-8322 or visit www .mysteryspotstignace.com. It sits on US Highway 2 West, 150 Martin Lake Road, five miles west of the Mackinac Bridge. Admission is charged for adults and children five years and older.

Taxidermy Heaven

Sault Ste. Marie

About a third of the way into my Paul Bunyan burger, an ear-piercing siren went off, causing me to nearly jump out of my seat. Blaring lights began to flash, screeching whistles blasted, and a voice came over the PA broadcasting "Welcome from Canada."

★ ★

Every mammal, fish, and reptile has more than its fill at Antler's.

It took a few seconds before I realized this was nothing more than a customary salutation from The Antler's Restaurant, one of many I'd hear before my last bite. Anyone can request a bells-and-whistles greeting. Although most are expressing good wishes for birthdays or anniversaries, one lucky guy heard the jolting news, "Congratulations, Darryl, the rabbit died."

Opening its doors first during Prohibition as the "Bucket-of-Blood Saloon and Ice Cream Parlor," the operation was brought to a halt when the IRS learned that profits of $900 were somehow accumulating on the sale of only one quart of ice cream a month. Rumor has it that "The Bucket" earned the distinction of becoming the first lemonade stand in history to refuse to sell to minors.

After the spot was purchased by two former Detroit policemen, Harold and Walt Kinney, in 1948, a new name went up over the entrance . . . ANTLER'S, for the three hundred mounts that eclipse the ceiling and walls. Over the bar you'll find six ducks a-flying, one swan a-swimming, and an anaconda slithered 'round a tree. Elsewhere, expect to encounter trophies of just about every creature that's walked, swum, or flown over the face of the earth, including wild boars, a deer, bison, lions, sharks, a full-sized polar beer, and a furry fish. A new species? The story goes that the water in nearby Lake Superior is so cold, even fish find it necessary to grow fur to survive.

The raucousness has brought in hungry revelers from every walk of life, including comedian Bob Goldthwait (who apparently wasn't recognized, since they put him on the waiting list), Motor City madman Ted Nugent, and Farrah Fawcett's mother (seated immediately). Back in the 1950s, when the Detroit Red Wings still spent summers training in the Sault, Antler's became known as the team's second home.

As I walked into the ladies' room, the doorway flocked with a deer's posterior, I was anxiously awaiting the clever displays I might find inside. To my disappointment, there were none. The only mount on the floral-papered walls was a vending machine dispensing Looney Tunes temporary tattoos.

Antler's Restaurant is open seven days a week. It's located at 804 East Portage Avenue; (906) 253-1728; www.saultantlers.com.

Putting the Word Out
Sault Ste. Marie

Writing anything about Lake Superior State University is enough to make a writer nervous. After all, this is the school that every year puts out a list of words they would like to see banished from the English language.

Get on the wrong side of the powers-that-be and I could become a wordless writer. Not unlike being a thoroughbred racehorse put out to stud after a vasectomy.

For twenty-six years Lake Superior State, a school known for a large male-to-female ratio and a great hockey program, has put out the "List of Words Banished from the Queen's English for Mis-use, Overuse, or General Uselessness." Every January 1 clichés and catchphrases are banished to the language junk heap they so richly deserve.

Over the years they've tried to exorcise such oxymoronic phrases as *free gift* in 1988, and *live audience* in 1983, 1987, and 1990. Proving that the mere posting on the list doesn't necessarily guarantee linguistic limbo.

The university accepts submissions from the populace at large, and the Public Relations Office gets an "overwhelming amount of submissions." (By the way, if you can be overwhelmed, how many other degrees of "whelme-dom" are there? Just asking, don't put me on the list!)

The 2001 list had a bumper crop courtesy of pundits, pollsters, and politicians. That year's terms included *fuzzy math, chads* of any type, and *negative growth*—which is the diametric opposite of *positive shrinking.*

Factoid made the list, as did *swipe,* as in approving a credit card. *Dotcom* is on the list but they don't care, because before long there aren't going to be enough of them around to complain.

In '02 *friendly fire* left, leaving one to ponder if unfriendly fire would be less painful, along with *reality TV, making money* (only counterfeiters make it; most honest people earn it), *foreseeable future* (as opposed to the unforeseeable future), and the weatherperson's crutch . . . *Doppler,* causing one Upper Peninsula station to invent its own recipe for "hobbler dobbler peach cobbler."

On the 2006 list was *a person of interest,* meaning either "people with guns want to talk to you" or the rest of us are too boring to talk to. That same year there was *an accident that didn't have to happen.* Does that mean some accidents need to happen?

In 2010 the word *czar* appeared with a long list of *shovel-ready* expressions. Maybe they developed an *app* for those who are addicted to *tweeting* or *sexting,* or for those who enjoy reading a *bromance* while they're *chillaxin'.* It seems like this list was just *too big to fail.* *Viral* took the top spot in 2011, while it's amazing that the word *amazing* didn't show up until 2012 when it entered at No. 1, followed by *baby bump* and *shared sacrifice,* making them the "new normal" for the list.

If you are interested in getting a word or phrase that has you ready to "go postal" (a previous winner), nominations for the future lists along with compelling reasons for banishment should be sent to: Word Banishment Public Relations Office, Lake Superior State University, Sault Ste. Marie, Michigan 49783. Or call (888) 800-LSSU, or visit www.lssu.edu/banished.

Push-a-Potty Parade
Trenary

The outhouse has been the butt of jokes for years. Recognizing this, the town of Trenary decided to heat up the dead of winter with their own form of bathroom humor. The Trenary Outhouse Classic is the brainchild of lifelong resident Toivo Aho . . . that's pronounced with a long *a.*

Sharon Fournier, secretary of the Outhouse Classic, says the rules are simple: Build an outhouse with wood and/or cardboard. Put in a toilet seat and a roll of toilet paper. Mount it on skis. Be the first to push it 500 feet and you're a winner.

Of course, creativity doesn't hurt. Since 1993 there have been some outrageous entries. Take, for instance, the White House Outhouse in 1999 with President Clinton sitting on the throne and Monica Lewinsky, walking by his side, attired in her infamous blue dress. Or in 2006, the Hot Toddy on the Potty.

A daffy duo from Munising has been among the biggest crowd-pleasers year after year.

Crowds check out Uncle Sam as he turns red, white, and blue in the face hoping for a heated cush for his tush in his outhouse on Constipation Avenue.

★ ★

Laurie Walsh and Marcy Heimerman put their two heads together and created the Vat I Can, themselves posing as nuns. Twelve months later they did quite an about-face, reemerging as the Pirates of the Carri pee an, complete with a peg leg that squirted yellow liquid.

Word of the unusual competition has spread nationwide, with contestants traveling from as far away as New York, Virginia, and North Carolina. All for a day guaranteed to provide a lot of laughs and maybe even some extra cash if you're one of the fastest pushers.

It's one big party, with the town of 550 swelling to more than 3,500 that last Saturday in February. Crowds line Main Street for the Privy Parade. When it's all done, mobs enjoy a game of volleyball in one of the huge snowbanks. Others may head over to the Silver Dollar or Trenary Tavern for a couple of pops.

If you're thinking of participating, you might want to bring along your golf shoes. It's not easy pushing an outhouse on ice, and those spikes may just come in handy to give you some much-needed traction.

For an application or to learn more about the hoity-toity event, call the Trenary Tavern at (906) 446-8305, write Outhouse Classic, PO Box 271, Trenary, Michigan 49891, or visit www.trenaryouthouseclassic .com. Of course, there are many "crappy" videos on YouTube . . .

Trenary Toast; Shelf Life—Eternity

Trenary

Forget about twice-baked potatoes. You haven't lived until you've tasted the popular twice-baked bread known as Trenary Toast. It's the creation of the Trenary Home Bakery, an establishment housed in its original building from 1930, although there have been several additions since to accommodate the growing demand for the UP staple.

The Siiranen family was the first owner; they sold it to Hans and Esther Hallinen in 1950, who've kept it in their family for three generations. Its current owner, grandson Joseph Hallinen, gives the real credit for twice-baked bread to the Vikings, who developed the technique centuries ago.

Staring at a plate of Trenary Toast can cause an
adrenaline rush for multitudes of hungry fans.

However, the recipe has remained the same. . . . Take sweet white
bread. Bake it. Add cinnamon and sugar. Bake it again.

Keep it in an airtight container and you can enjoy it forever. Or
almost. Even though the official guarantee is for six months, it's been
known to last for years. On Day 1,274 it tastes exactly as it did on Day 1.

On your first bite, you'll say it's hard. It's supposed to be. Think of it
as a Finnish biscotti, and use it to dunk in your coffee.

People all over the country enjoy the toasty treat, with 3,000 bags
going out weekly. A ten-ounce bag containing ten to fourteen pieces
will set you back $3.45.

The Trenary Home Bakery ships to all fifty states, but does supply some retail outlets in lower Michigan. And no, they don't use any pre-servatives; the trick is all in the baking. You can visit them at E2918 Highway 67. Dial (906) 446-3330 or (800) 862-7801 (TOAST01), or log on to www.trenarytoast.us. Open Monday through Friday 9:00 a.m. to 7:00 p.m., Saturday and Sunday 10:00 a.m. to 3:00 p.m.

Davey Jones Locker of the Great Lakes
Whitefish Point

Opening the doors, the first poignant strains of Gordon Lightfoot's version of "The Edmund Fitzgerald" can be heard breaking through. Your eyes hone in a large brass bell, emblazoned with the words EDMUND FITZGERALD, retrieved almost twenty years to the date after the mighty freighter sank in the waters of Lake Superior just seventeen miles from where you now stand.

It is to this and the other 6,000 ships lost on the Great Lakes that the Shipwreck Museum at Whitefish Point pays tribute. Thirteen differ-ent shipwrecks are recapped—no explanation for the odd number—ranging from the *Invincible* in 1816 to the *Fitzgerald*'s 1975 demise. Selected artifacts from each are displayed: hats, glasses, binoculars, even a gold wedding ring, telling their own tales of the eighty-mile area just outside what's come to be known as "Shipwreck Coast" due, in part, to the perpetually high winds and treacherous weather conditions.

On a somewhat brighter note, the museum is filled with magnifi-cent shadows cast off the 344 crystal prisms of the bigger-than-life Fresnel lens. Each is so precisely arranged that even a modest source of light is refracted into an intense beam visible for more than twenty-eight miles.

A somewhat daunting and thought-provoking afternoon can be spent inside, pondering the two questions that have never been answered: Why did the lighthouse fail to shine on November 10, 1975, the night the *Fitzgerald* and her twenty-nine-member crew went

A seventeen-foot-tall Fresnel lens with a range of twenty-eight miles stands guard over the actual bell retrieved from the *Edmund Fitzgerald.*

down? And why did it go out again on July 4, 1995, the night the divers returned with her bell?

For a true feel of the mystery surrounding Whitefish Point, you can spend a night in the crew members' quarters, built in 1923. Fully renovated, rooms are $150 a night and are available April 1 through November 14. For reservations, call (888) 492-3747. Follow Highway 123 to its northernmost end; a dirt road will lead you the rest of the way.

The museum, including a fascinating video and tour of the lighthouse, is open daily, May 1 through October 31. Admission is charged. For more info, call toll-free (800) 635-1742 or visit their website, www .shipwreckmuseum.com.

7

The Middle Fingers

Please note that the chapter is "Middle Fingers," with an s, plural, more than one. This is an expansive area of Michigan, protruding to the northernmost tip of the Lower Peninsula incorporating index, ring, and, yes, middle finger. This is the region most commonly thought of when you hear people say they're going "up north," allowing room for some crossover into the pinkie.

Prime deer hunting territory, each November, Interstate 75 (aka speed trap heaven) jams up with more camouflage outfits than the US Army, on their way to combat duty in the woods. Year-round, waterways, too, are filled with those setting their sights on nabbing the big one that got away.

Yes, we do love our animals, if only to admire them from afar. The state's biggest elk population resides in Otsego and Montmorency Counties, and while there are no pigeons in Pigeon River, you're more likely to catch a glimpse of a sturgeon in Black Lake than you are on Sturgeon River.

It's a safe bet that this is the only place in the world where you can walk inside a dinosaur, pork out on the golf course, and come face to face with a man-killing clam. You have to be in tip-top physical condition merely to be an onlooker at one of the annual sporting events here.

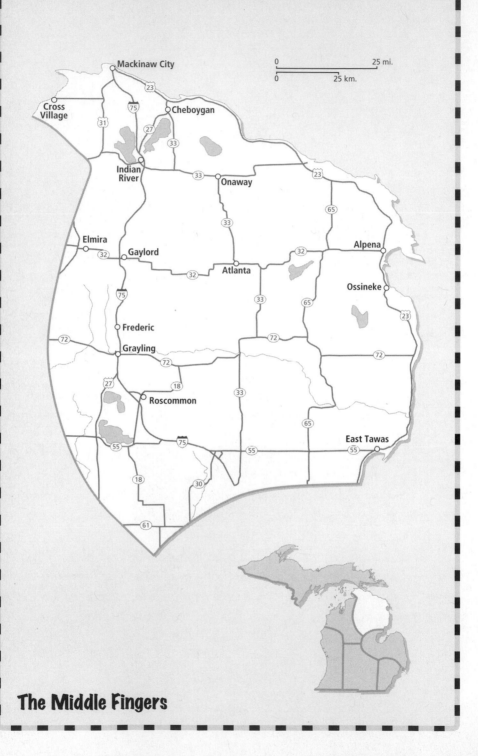

The Middle Fingers

The Middle Fingers

★ ★

Gene Taylor made his second home in this region—fondly labeled "the Sunrise Side"— where he savored the splendor of radiant morning skies as only a true morning person could do.

Contrary to Charlie Brown's saying "Morning people are hard to love," after experiencing the delightful idiosyncrasies of the people, places, and things of Michigan's northeast, before long, it will be obvious why each new dawn is blithely greeted with a three (middle) finger salute.

★ ★

One Man's Junk is Another College's Mascot

Alpena

Talk about taking recycling to new heights. On the campus of Alpena Community College stands a thirty-foot merger of vintage car parts and a legendary woodsman. This funky and fun sculpture of Paul Bunyan comes from the junkyards of Detroit, with a body created from fenders and hoods of the Kaiser, an automobile which stopped production in the 1950s.

Michigan artist Betty Conn is Kaiser Paul's birth mother, assisted by welder Edward X. Tuttle. Before assembling their baby boy, the old auto parts were handled with tender, loving care to ensure longevity. Each part was sandblasted and primed, and once joined together, the inside of the structure was sprayed with a rust-proofing compound.

Instead of a beauty shop, Paul was coiffed in a machine shop, where his curly hair and beard were custom-designed from extra-coarse steel shavings.

The $4,500 creative pile of auto junk has led a rather peripatetic lifestyle. Born in the 1960s, Paul was first perched on the roof of the Paul Bunyan Gas Station on Main Street in Gaylord. (As Mama Conn put her son's fenders in place, she caused more than one fender bender herself, standing on a ladder in her fashionably short "short-shorts.") After a dozen years, the station folded, and the wood-chopping giant was transported a few hundred feet to stand in front of the Indian Museum. A year later the museum closed, and for the next eighteen years Paul resided in front of Grayling's AuSable-Manistee Realty.

When the realty office closed, the question became: "What do you do with a thirty-foot-tall metal lumberjack?" The logical answer? Alpena Community College. After all, the official mascot of the men's basketball team just happened to be a lumberjack. In 1998, thanks to a flatbed truck, Paul was able to be transported in one piece, and along with a group of students who did some much-needed sandblasting and repainting, he was looking as good as new in no time.

The auto industry could learn a lesson from this Paul Bunyan.
JAY WALTERREIT

Today he stands upright on campus near the gymnasium, hoping for his sake, and that of the Kaiser, that this will become his final resting place.

Pay a visit to Alpena Community College with long, tall Paul, at 666 Johnson Street, Alpena. For more information call the campus at (989) 356-9021 or (888) 468-6222.

★ ★

Ham It Up and Out
Atlanta

Michiganians are the biggest swingers in the country. Now don't get teed off by that statement until you hear all the facts. According to statistics from the National Golf Foundation, the mitten state has the nation's highest percentage of residents over the age of twelve who play the frustrating "chase-the-little-white-ball" game. Yep, 20 percent of all Michiganians hit the links, or the sand traps, or other things they're not aiming for. And if you need to know how you fare against a typical golfer, that's been defined as a just-over-forty-year-old male who plays twenty-two rounds per year, shooting an average of 97.

Stepping out of character is the tenth hole of Elk Ridge Golf Club, a 450-acre public course designed by Michigan architect Jerry Matthews. From the tip of the tees to the tip of the green there's an elevation change of 100 feet, providing panoramic views of the north and an increased opportunity for nosebleeds. What uniquely marks this hole is the front right bunker, a real bear to get out of, as the sand appears ready to snort from its shapely snout. Your vision's fine: Staring you in the face is the shapely physique of a pig. Not a wild boar, but a Porky-style pig.

Always good for a few laughs, foursomes have been known to bet against the squiggly tail—whoever hits into it buys everyone a round of . . . ham sandwiches.

The pig's existence is courtesy of Lou Schmidt, who as owner of both the course and the Honey Baked Ham Company has proven he's not only a fanatical golfer but also a bona fide publicity ham.

For nongolfers, pig viewings are available from the tepee-style clubhouse at Elk Ridge Golf Club, 9400 Rouse Road, six miles north of Atlanta off Highway 33. Call (989) 785-2275 or (800) 626-4355, or visit www.elkridgegolf.com.

★ ★

Kingfish of Kitsch

Cheboygan

Leslie Earl: She sells seashells, not by the sea, but right off Interstate 75, at exit 326. The unlikely location of this oceanic emporium known as Sea Shell City has been wooing devotees since 1957. As only the second proprietor in its nearly half-century history, Earl doesn't seem fazed that this tropical merchandising paradise sits in the heart of northern Michigan. After all, "Not everyone can go to Florida, so they come here instead."

Leslie Earl could have easily shelled out a clambake for the entire population of Michigan with this 505-pound beauty.

★ ★

Almost as well known as the business itself are the eleven billboards lining the preceding forty-mile stretch of freeway, with adrenaline-rushing captions STOP AND SEE CAPTAIN HOOK, ONE MILLION SHELLS, and the clincher . . . FREE ADMISSION TO VIEW THE GIANT MAN-KILLING CLAM.

Once inside the 8,000-square-foot, meticulously maintained galley of gifts, the assortment is wider than the Atlantic and Pacific combined. Shoppers weave through aisles filled with unrelated trinkets: nautical

Wanted: Sturgeon-Sitters, No Experience Necessary

In these parts they take their sturgeon seriously, and for good reason. With its prehistoric origins, some say looking into the eyes of the largest freshwater fish anywhere is like looking into the eyes of a dinosaur. It's a threatened species, and Cheboygan's determined to do whatever it takes to preserve the eight-foot, 200-pound centurions that make their home in Black Lake.

A round-the-clock sturgeon protection program during spawning season has 350 volunteers who spend 3,800 hours wrapped in blankets at night with video cameras in hand, guarding the fish from those who want to poach the eggs for caviar. Maybe not the most exciting line of work, but at least the fish don't talk back or give you trouble at bedtime.

novelties, T-shirts espousing the benefits of Michigan roadkill, sponges, Gummi Sharks, and rows and rows of bins hemorrhaging every type of shell ever known to sand.

A few feet beyond the saltwater aquarium is the proclaimed pièce de résistance . . . the mammoth clam. Yes, it's a real clam, though it hasn't been alive in at least fifty years. Purchased in the Philippines, it weighs in at 505 pounds and—though I hate to disillusion you—couldn't possibly

Then, in what could be considered a paradoxical move, each February since 1948 about 1,000 people wait in line for one of the twenty-five daily sturgeon tags that come available. A lottery decides the chosen few who will venture out on the ice for a chance to spear one of the five fish they've been licensed to kill.

So how long does it take to capture five struggling sturgeons? In 2002 it took a full twelve days. In 2011, the season opened and closed on the same day with 330 anglers capturing the quota in just four hours. That year's catch ranged from twenty-nine to sixty-eight inches with weights from five to seventy-three pounds. But the record was set in 2001. With barely enough time to lace up your boots, the quintet was rounded up in just thirty-five minutes.

For more information on any of the sturgeon programs, contact the Sturgeon General, Brenda Archambo, through the website www .sturgeonfortomorrow.org.

have devoured anyone. Clams are vegetarians. But you'll never see one bigger. That is, unless you're the culprit who a few years ago took the 700-pounder out of the parking lot.

Sea Shell City, at exit 326 off Interstate 75, will occupy more than a few minutes, giving the kids a chance to stretch their legs on the pirate ship outside. It's open from the third week in March through the third weekend in October, seven days a week, 9:00 a.m. to 5:00 p.m. Call (877) 435-5248 or hook on at www.seashellcitymi.com.

Legs Still Standing Thanks to Polish Indian Chief
Cross Village

Na zdrowie! Those were the words spoken in 1921 by a thirty-four-year-old Polish immigrant as he raised his glass in a toast to his new neighbors, the Ottawa Indians of Cross Village. The bonds of brotherhood grew strong, and the local tribe's chief, having no male heirs, took in Stanley Smolak as one of his own, bestowing upon him the Indian name of Chief White Cloud.

In gratitude for the wonder and beauty of his adopted land, Chief Smolak used his dexterity to build the two-story Legs Inn, a feat accomplished with only his two hands and all the stumps, limbs, roots, and stones that nature could provide. With one exception . . . the legs. They're actually legs of stoves, which he inverted to form the decorative railing on the roof. Hence the name *Legs Inn,* although it might be better suited to *Legs Up.*

The extraordinary complex is operated today as a restaurant by Stanley's nephew, George Smolak, and his wife, Kathy, serving up helpings of golabki, pierogi, lasanki, and bigos (a Polish hunter's stew), which you can wash down with one of a hundred different beers. Of course, if you're worried about your Polish pronunciation you can always order the cheese nachos.

It may seem a little odd at first to see someone from Italy or Taiwan in a traditional Polish costume walk up and ask you if you'd like some nalesnik, but Legs proudly participates in an International Cultural

Struggle is the unusual name given to one of the
unique woodcarvings lining the interior of Legs Inn.

Exchange Program, exposing all nations to a taste of the Polish side of Michigan.

This is the one place where you actually hope there is a line to get in, so you can linger in the manicured gardens where the view over Lake Michigan is as close to heaven as you're likely to get on earth. Time it right and you'll catch a captivating sunset that's more than worth the wait. Or better yet, try to get one of the dining tables outside and then raise your glass in a "Hail to Chief Smolak." *Smacznego!*

Getting to Legs Inn from Harbor Springs is a memorable drive through Highway 119's "Tunnel of Trees." It's located in the heart of Cross Village at 6425 Lake Shore Drive; there are no reservations. Open mid-May through the third week in October for lunch and dinner. Phone (231) 526-2281 or visit www.legsinn.com.

Stan the Man
East Tawas

He's there when they open. He's there when they close. He doesn't cause any problems and nobody ever has to drive him home. At Mr. Jack'ss Sports Bar and Grill in East Tawas, you might call Stan the perfect regular. Stan loved the gang at what was formerly called Chum's and wasn't about to let a little thing like dying get in the way of hanging out there. When Stan finally got the ultimate last call December 5, 1998, it seemed only fitting that part of his ashes ended up in an empty bottle of his beloved Imperial whiskey in a place of honor behind the bar.

John and Glenda Revord owned Chum's, a local watering hole that's been around for nearly sixty years. These days the tourists are more likely to order a margarita or ask to see the wine list than the Imperial whiskey on the rocks that Stan Humphrey favored. When Stan dropped by Chum's after a day of selling used cars at his lot on US Highway 23, there weren't the touches that you see now: the espresso machine that's just a short distance from his perch, the electronic darts game, the big-screen TV, or the bottles of Chambord or

✦ ✦

Godiva chocolate liqueur. Back when he first came in, Stan was lucky to get popcorn as opposed to the "Acorn squash–covered Chicken" or "Kathy's Krab Sandwich" that are on the menu now.

In 1920 half of Chum's was Aunt Fran's Lunch Counter. She sold it in 1930 to her brother Chumie Kleanow. In 1933 when Prohibition ended, the bar got one of the earliest liquor licenses issued by the state (it has zeros in front of the number). Chumie rented out the bar to various operators until 1946, when it was Rita's Place. She got into a disagreement with the liquor commission, who forced her to sell it. It became Chum's that year. Even now there's a 1948 phone book on the wall at Chum's, and because everybody had the same exchange in town, some of the phone numbers are only one digit. Chumie ran the bar until his death in 1956, when it was taken over by his son Billy Kleanow.

Stan Humphrey saw it all. Stan hailed from Hale, Michigan, a short distance across Highway 55, and he started stopping by Chum's in 1934 at the age of eighteen (liquor laws weren't quite as strict in those days). His work schedule permitted him to stop by the bar when things were slow at the used-car lot, and the word was that Stan probably sold as many cars out of "Chum's branch office" as he did at the dealership.

After he retired, Stan stopped by Chum's every morning to make sure everything was right with the world, had a couple of drinks, and then headed out until he returned for cocktail hour about 4:30. He became so much a part of the Chum's family that when it was suggested the place wanted some of his ashes as a tribute after he retired to that long bar in the sky, Stan said, "Ask the kids." When they approved, a shrine was born.

When Chum's was sold on May 1, 2009, to Marty Rogers, Stan became part of the deal. Rogers wants the story to live and felt it was his duty to keep Stan in the bottle where he's been for years. He's become a celebrity in his own right with people stopping by to say hello and have a shot of Imperial in his honor. Every year in mid-July,

Stan Humphrey never leaves the bar, even at closing time. His remains sit inside this bottle of Imperial whiskey on a shelf at Mr. Jack'ss Sports Bar and Grill.

HELEN PASAKARNIS

* ★

Stan's family and friends gather in East Tawas for a golf outing and party in Stan's honor. But nobody at Mr. Jack'ss ever has to worry about things getting out of control. After all, kids know to behave when their dad is in the room.

Mr. Jack'ss Sports Bar and Grill is located at 105 West Westover; (989) 305-6506.

One Potato, Two Potato, Burgers for All
Elmira

It's a convenient way to get three and a half weeks' worth of your body's nutritional requirements for carbohydrates and cholesterol. Two or three bites max of the state's only potato burger should do the trick.

Now, a potato burger wouldn't be my first choice if it were buried in the middle of the menu. However, the Railside Bar and Grill, formerly the Elmira Inn, is the home of the original potato burger so it seemed foolish not to give it a try. I wasn't disappointed, but give my gastrointestinal tract a few hours to respond.

The potato burger is the invention of Elmira's Ellen Czykoski. She's one of twenty-three children, perhaps precipitating her creative culinary talents. Her recipe consists of taking a concoction of shredded potatoes, ground beef, and seasonings, pre-frying it so the whole thing doesn't fall apart, dipping it in beer batter, and finally submerging it full throttle into the deep-fryer before it's slapped on a bun. Guaranteed to clog even the cleanest arteries.

Thanks to bikers, both peddlers and motored, who crave their carbs, after a recent marathon the cash register rang up a belly-busting two hundred PBs in one day, leaving one to wonder if folks were totally "mashed" when they left.

A potato burger with cheese and fries goes for $7.99. Unless you're famished, share it with a friend. Railside Bar and Grill is on Highway 32, two miles east of US Highway 131 on the south side of the road. The official address is 501 Underwood, though that's the side street and there isn't a side door. Phone (231) 546-3248. Open every day.

★ ★

Fred Bear's All to Local Collector
Frederic

Pete Kocefas switches hats faster than a juggler in a three-ring circus.
One minute he's answering his phone "Sledhead's Snowmobiles"; the
next it's "First Impressions"—his sign company; or he could be greeting the caller with "Wayside Inn Cottage," a rental property. Summing
it up best are the words inscribed on one of the many posters he has
of his hero, FRED BEAR—RESTLESS SPIRIT.

The Grayling area has been having a love fest with Fred Bear and
his archery equipment ever since his manufacturing plant went up in
1939, when it employed some four hundred people. Almost everyone
in town was involved with the company in one way or another, and
there were dark clouds overhead that dismal day in 1978 when the
operations were transferred to Florida. The Fred Bear Museum continued to operate for two years beyond that before tearfully shutting its
doors locally, too. With a worldwide reputation, people to this day still
stop and ask how to find it.

That's why Kocefas stepped in, to continue paying tribute to the
man who used to walk the downtown streets daily and stop and talk
to anyone he passed. It started out as a collection of a few bows, but
word spread quickly; and it wasn't long before anyone in Grayling who
found something of Bear's in a closet would instantly cry out, "Call
Pete." A sampling of newly acquired pieces occupies a corner of Kocefas's snowmobile shop. One of the first Fred Bear Museum T-shirts sits
folded in its original plastic wrapper with a price tag of $5.50. That's
what it cost years ago—none of the collection is for sale today, nor
will it ever be, as the hobby is strictly an expression of respect and
admiration.

While several bows hang out in easy eyesight, the larger "shrine" is
set up in the back workroom. Here you'll find another 150 arrow pro-
pellers artistically surrounding numerous Fred Bear posters, a feather
barrel (the contents remain untouched), and hundreds of trinkets ranging from Fred's own hatpin collection to his personal hunting knife

A shrine to archery icon Fred Bear.

crafted in Africa, covered in nothing less than lion fur. Recent acquisi-
tions include a pair of Fred Bear coveralls and a Fred Bear signature
bow (a big deal, at least to Kocefas).

Always on the lookout for anything that Bear ever touched, one day
Kocefas and his nine-year-old daughter were doing their own excava-
tion of the site of the bygone museum when she frustratingly asking,
"Dad, you're not thinking of getting that toilet seat?" Up popped a
scheming twinkle in his eye, leaving one to only imagine what happened next.

Kocefas is always willing to share his enthusiasm with interested parties. Most winter days you can catch him at Sledhead's, 6636 North Old 27. Otherwise his sign states, SUMMER HOURS BY APPOINTMENT OR WHEN MY VAN IS HERE. Call him at (989) 344-7669—that's (989) 344-DIGSNOW—or visit www.sledheadsusa.com.

Tree "Weights" for Winter to Spring to Life
Gaylord

Typically in Michigan, the greenery sheds its summer skin thus lightening its load in anticipation of the stagnant months ahead. Not so for one tree in Gaylord—a tree that really doesn't come to life until the first freeze.

No one knows exactly how or when the Gaylord Ice Tree, as it's become commonly known, first got started. As many people say, "When life hands you lemons, make lemonade." Here they say, "When Michigan hands you cold weather, make an ice tree." Which is exactly what they've been doing now for more than sixty years.

Before the onset of winter, a three-story gangly metal structure resembling an anorexic pyramid is erected on the front lawn of the City County Building. There it sits until the temperatures get bitterly cold, possibly sometime in August, at which time a sort of metallurgic proctologist is called in to work his magic. A watering rod is rammed through the midsection running up to the top. The pipes are cleaned and the floodgates are let loose.

The tree then gets a nice, steady shower of warm water (officials say heated water freezes faster) continuing round-the-clock for months, frosting the structure with frozen prisms, providing, in a manner of speaking, "the icing on the tree."

Of course Mother Nature can't guarantee uniformity, so each annual creation is truly one-of-a-kind. At its peak, the tree glaciates to about twenty feet with a girth of twenty-two feet, tipping the scales at approximately 245 tons.

The ultimate meltdown—240 tons and still losing.

And, yes, there have been times where the tree has been on thin ice. Leaning toward being top heavy, a few times it's toppled over, once almost hitting the county judge in his office.

Yet, all in all, it could be the best government value anywhere. Word is that the cost of the ice tree for an entire season, including the structure and umpteen thousand gallons of water, is only $200.

The Gaylord City County Building sits on the 45th parallel at 225 West Main Street. The Gaylord Convention and Tourist Bureau can answer your questions at (989) 732-4000 or (800) 345-8621. Their website is www.gaylordmichigan.net/ice-tree--22, which will also lead you to their 24/7 ice tree webcam—just don't expect much in the summer.

Coca-Cola Splashed Everywhere, Floor to Ceiling
Grayling

The loudspeaker on the roof of Dawson and Stevens Restaurant is blaring the voice of Dion singing "Runaround Sue," setting the stage for the high dose of nostalgia you'll find inside. This eatery is now a classic '50s diner, with an original soda fountain that dates back to 1938.

Current owner, Bill Gannon, was on a roll when he purchased the business in 2004. After a brief renovation, he was looking for ways to bring in more customers and wound up buying the entire 10,000-item Coca-Cola collection—known for more than a decade as the Bottle Cap Museum—from nearby Sparr resident Bill Hicks.

Today, every available square inch is filled with 100 percent authentic antiques . . . no reproductions here. Among the assortment, you'll find original Coca-Cola hats, bow ties, a musical cigarette lighter, dolls, vintage posters, and, of course, bottle caps, dating back to the early 1800s. Even the restrooms are jammed with collectibles . . . the men's room with Coca-Cola Nascar posters, the women's room with puzzles and a changing table doubling as a display case packed with trademark stuffed animals and toys.

No matter how hard you look, there's no sign of Pepsi here.

Gannon's sister, Marianne McEvoy, is the curator of more than 15,000 pieces of memorabilia, which she rotates from storage on a weekly basis.

The 110-seat eating area is the real thing, too. You won't see a terrazzo floor like that in new buildings. And how many counters today have a hook designed especially to hang your purse or package?

Besides the intriguing decor, the food will make you want to dance with mashed potatoes, Soldier Boy (reuben), and the Betty Boop Cherry Chicken Salad Melt.

It's all fun and a trip down memory lane. You can twist and shout and fill your tummy at Dawson and Stevens at 231 E. Michigan Avenue; (989) 348-2111; www.bottlecapmuseum.com.

This Sport's a Hoot for Night Owls
Grayling

On Saturday, September 6, 1947, the Au Sable River gave birth to a set of twins: the world's longest marathon canoe race and the world's toughest spectator sport. No one was quite ready for the second seed to become as prominent as it has, but for more than fifty-five years now, thousands of people have been following two-person teams paddling 120 miles nonstop from Grayling to Oscoda. A perfect outlet for

Thousands of fans line the banks of the Au Sable to catch a fleeting glimpse of the fleet of paddlers.
GRAYLING REGIONAL CHAMBER OF COMMERCE AND GRAYLING AREA VISITORS COUNCIL

insomniacs, the competition begins at 9:00 p.m. and runs for fourteen to nineteen straight hours.

And what a beginning it is. With a hundred participants all lined up, ten feet apart, the cannon explodes, signaling a run-for-your-life mad dash toward the narrow (just twenty feet) opening of the river, while crowds scream wildly on shore.

All night long the excited devotees line the banks of the river to cheer for the athletes, who come from twenty-two different states and at least one foreign country. It's hard to tell who's in better shape since top-notch strength and stamina are requirements for involvement on either side of this marathon. Instead of late-night bar-hopping, it's bridge-hopping that's going on with an equal amount of rowdiness.

The course itself isn't easy even in daylight, with many obstacles to circumvent including six dams, each forcing paddlers out of their boats to sprint over uneven, slippery terrain. So the teams' bank runners come equipped with everything from bandages to flashlights to duct tape (which has been used on several occasions to mend a boo-booed boat).

No matter what the outcome, it's always wildly fun and rewarding recreation; those who participate once say it's hard not to experience it again. Just ask Al Widing Sr. from Mio, and his crewmate, Rick Joy of Lapeer County. In 2011, individually they completed the race a record-setting thirty-one times. Joy, at age fifty-six, and Widing, at eighty-six, took their team to fortieth place out of ninety-four entries.

The race is now held the last weekend in July. Information is available by calling (989) 348-4425 or visiting their website at www.a usablecanoemarathon.org. The countdown clock tells you how much time you have left to get into condition.

Cross in the Woods
Indian River

Throughout this and many books like it, you'll find "The World's Largest This" or "That." It's not the size of the world's largest crucifix in Indian River, Michigan, that impresses, however; it's the aura about it.

The world's largest crucifix, created by
Michigan sculptor Marshal Fredericks, attracts
visitors from all corners of the globe.

That aura is one reason that the cross has attracted millions of visitors of all faiths from around the world.

On June 26, 1946, the first Mass was celebrated at the newly established Indian River parish. The priest there got the idea to build an outdoor shrine after reading about the Blessed Kateri Tekakwitha. It was her practice to place crosses throughout the woods. The Indian maiden born in 1656 converted to Christianity at the age of eighteen. Her crosses were outdoor mini chapels for prayer. She was sort of the spiritual Johnny Appleseed who gave Father Charles Brophy the idea for an outdoor shrine featuring a large wooden cross as the centerpiece.

In 1954 a fifty-five-foot cross made of one redwood tree was erected. In 1959 a seven-ton bronze likeness of Jesus was added, making it the world's largest crucifix. Located just two minutes off Interstate 75 at exit 310, the cross was a popular stop for tourists heading up to the Upper Peninsula. In 1983 there was a complete renovation of the outdoor area, including the altar, the Stations of the Cross, and the Shrine of the Madonna of the Highway. The grounds also include a shrine to St. Francis of Assisi, founder of the Franciscans, one of the largest orders in the Roman Catholic Church.

For the first fifty years of the shrine's existence, any extended stay was possible only during the spring-through-fall seasons because the location in Michigan's northern snow belt made midwinter visits impossible. That problem was rectified on June 29, 1997, when the new church was dedicated; now visitors can spend time at the cross 365 days a year. There are daily services inside the church year-round and outdoor services in summer.

You'll find the Cross in the Woods at 7078 Highway 68. Contact (213) 238-8973 or visit www.crossinthewoods.com.

Sisters Who Are Habit Forming
Indian River

It's 8:00 a.m. and 525 sisters are faithfully lined up, properly attired in starched collars, and ready to meet their adoring public. Shhh . . .

The habits of 525 religious orders in both North and
South America grace the halls of the Nun Doll Museum.

★ ★

silence is the golden rule here. Not a sound is uttered as they all conduct themselves as perfect dolls. The doors are opening for the day at the Nun Doll Museum.

"Michigan's best-kept secret" started as a private collection. You might think it belonged to a modest Catholic girl aspiring to one day enter the convent . . . but instead it was Sally Rogalski, a young Lutheran, who came up with the idea of dressing her dolls as nuns in thanksgiving for the life-saving care her mother had received from the Daughters of Charity.

Sally converted, married, and her hobby grew into a habit she just couldn't kick. In 1967, out of gratitude for additional favors received, she and her late husband, Wally, decided to present a few of the dolls to Indian River's Cross in the Woods. Today there are hundreds of them, some even life sized, representing the detailed garb of religious orders the world over, many dressed by the nuns themselves. In 1988 Pope John Paul II issued an official proclamation recognizing the Rogalskis and their Nun Doll Museum as the largest such collection anywhere.

And since confession is good for the soul, it's time to 'fess up. There aren't 525 sisters. Included in that number is a priest in his robes, because, as Sally says, "He should be there."

The Nun Doll Museum is open daily. The Rogalskis have stated that there will never be a charge for admission. It's located on Highway 68, exit 310 off Interstate 75. For more info call (231) 238-8973 or visit www.crossinthewoods.com and click on Nun Doll Museum.

Keys "Hole Up" in Unlikely Spot
Mackinaw City

How many times have you caught yourself saying "Where did I leave my keys?" If you're in Mackinaw City, the likely answer is The Key Hole Bar and Grill, an unpretentious watering hole and eatery that has permanently adopted more than 17,000 keys.

It's not as unlikely a home for keys as one might initially think. Picture yourself sitting at one of their five keyhole-shaped bars. After a

The secret ingredient of this "keychyn's" success may
be the hundreds of motel keys hovering overhead.
DIANA NOWAK

drink or two, you reach in your pocket and discover an old key that no
longer has anything to unlock. You shrug your shoulders and hand it
over to the bartender.

Owner Sharon Zulski says the almost-daily practice has been going
on even before she came on board more than thirty years ago. The
building dates back to 1893 and over the years has changed names a
number of times, yet the keys remain. Car keys . . . railroad keys . . .
padlocks with their keys . . . they're all here, filling up every inch of
available space.

The "treasured" keys, those from old motels on their original keychain, hang over the main bar. Close inspection discovers those that at one time unlocked the finest hotels in Europe, Ireland, Poland, Rio de Janeiro, and Bolivia, though Zulski adds, "Don't expect to come in, grab a key, and get a free room somewhere." The keys have been here so long, either the places are out of business or they've changed their security systems.

Capitalizing on the theme is "key" to the success of the business. Even before you enter, you'll notice the oversized keyhole on the front door. Inside, colorful stained glass is patterned in key configurations. The menu features Master, Dexter, and Yale submarine sandwiches.

It's good food and good fun, with perhaps a bit of therapy thrown in. At least it was for one new divorcee, who, when handing over his key exclaimed, "This is the key to the house my ex-wife just got."

The Key Hole Bar and Grill is located at 323 East Central Avenue, Mackinaw City; (231) 436-7911. Open seven days a week.

Sorry, Plymouth, America's Founding Rock Lives Here
Mackinaw City

Thanksgiving would be a far different holiday if McGulpin Rock got the credit it's due. It's true that the Pilgrims landed at Plymouth Rock in 1620. But it was a full five years before that when Etienne Brule and a band of French explorers became the first group of Europeans to cross all the Great Lakes. Their trusty navigational guide through the Straits of Mackinac was none other than a massive boulder at least five times bigger than the much more famous rock in Massachusetts.

Historians believe that McGulpin Rock was revered far before its 1615 discovery. There's evidence that Native American Indians used it to keep track of the ever-changing water levels in Lake Michigan, important knowledge when you're paddling a canoe across the Straits. Later, in 1749, it was listed on the first map of the Great Lakes, helping the cruising maneuvers of the French at Fort Michilimackinac.

Size matters and at nine feel tall, with a vertical circumference of thirty-seven feet, horizontal circumference of 33.8 feet, and weighing fifty-four tons, the rock served as a sort of visual GPS marker. That's compared to Plymouth Rock, which weighed a mere ten tons, eventually split apart, and now sits encased under protective covering.

McGulpin Rock continues to stand strong, facing the elements for centuries au naturel. It presents a picturesque setting with the magnificent Mackinac Bridge as a backdrop.

So why—with its significant value and beauty—don't people know about McGulpin Rock? Why isn't it mentioned in textbooks? Why don't people acknowledge that the Straits of Mackinac played a major part in the founding of America? Michigan historians speculate that it's because the landing involved the French, rather than the British. Ultimately it was the English who wrote all of the early history books. If life was fair, our Thanksgiving tables might be featuring duck a l'orange, crepes, and crème brûlée.

McGulpin Rock is located adjacent to Headlands Recreational Park, west of Mackinaw City. Since this rock doesn't have an address or a phone, it's best to use that of the McGulpin Lighthouse, 500 Headlands Drive; (231) 436-5860. You can drive right down to the lake for a world-class photo op.

His Patriotism Isn't Just Another Fabrication
Onaway

By day, Tom Moran is the president and CEO of Moran Ironworks, an industrial repair company specializing in structural steel for hospitals and schools. At night, he releases his pent up creative juices and transforms himself into a master metal sculptor.

An extremely talented welder with the "best-looking ductwork anywhere," Moran realized there "was something inside that needed to come out." So he started showing his patriotic side, producing bigger-than-life artistic works for the local Fourth of July parade. He says a twelve-by-twelve-foot bust of George Washington "kept me out

* *

Taking patriotism to new heights.
TOM BEELER

of the bars" for 1,000 hours on nights and weekends and now sits in a field next to his house for all to enjoy, even the "hobo who slept underneath it for a few nights."

At last count Moran had produced twenty super-sized structures, from the fourteen-foot brass, stainless steel, and copper eagle's head sitting on the lawn of the Onaway Court House to the massive Liberty Bell at the local VFW hall. Rogers City has his version of the Statue of Liberty. His "Wal-Mart version" of an 18,000-pound Indian Head sits in the Michigan Magazine Museum in Comins.

Then there are the "working" sculptures. In 1995 it was a fully operational fourteen-foot water pump. Before that there was a 5,000-pound V-8 powered chainsaw, now outside Da Yooper Tourist Trap in Ishpeming.

The *Guinness Book of World Records* credited him in 1992 with the largest pick ax, measuring thirty-six feet.

Moran has never left his hometown of Onaway, yet in some ways he epitomizes the phrase, "You've come a long way baby." When he started out in 1978, he was a one-man welding and fabrication show, operating out of a rented garage. At last count, he had nearly fifty employees working out of his own 60,000-square-foot building.

He has an unwritten rule that his works should be at least a mile apart. You can view them throughout Onaway. To check out his not-so-mini version of Mt. Rushmore, go a half mile west of town on Highway 33. You can't miss it. Washington's profile is best viewed from an angle. Head on he's been confused with Thomas Jefferson, Marlon Brando, and Pink Floyd.

For more info Moran Ironworks is at 11739 Highway 68/33 in Onaway. Call (989) 733-2011 or visit www.moraniron.com and click on Community Artwork for a real treat.

Still Life in Jurassic Park
Ossineke

Dinosaurs were hip and cool in Ossineke long before that larger-than-life purple "I love you—you love me" Barney was even a glimmer in his parents' carnivorous eye. Paul Domke, back in 1934, for some unknown reason fell under the spell of the giant terrestrials. Once hooked, he stopped at nothing to share his fascination with the rest of Michigan.

From his own home-brewed recipe, he sculpted dinosaurs with life-sized dimensions and didn't stop for the next forty years, until twenty-six had been meticulously crafted. Not just mammoth outlines, each creature is prehistorically correct right down to the muscular tendons.

★ ★

With a vision of engaging the public with Tyrannosaurus rex and iguanodon, Dinosaur Gardens Prehistorical Zoo was created—forty eerie acres of swampy land a la Jurassic Park.

Here's a chance to get up close and personal with the big boys, even exploring the guts inside. Those inviting steps coming out of the apotosaurus's side take you on a journey of discovery to find, instead of the heart, a figure of Jesus. Is it any coincidence that the body of running water here is "Devil River"?

Whatever you conclude, it's a thought-provoking mile-long hike that weaves you through the towering four-legged beasts with titil-lating tidbits: Did you know that the stegosaurus had two brains, one—the size of a walnut—to operate his jaws and front legs, and the other, twenty times larger, controlling the action of his backside? I think we all know someone who similarly has predominant intelligence in the posterior.

Dinosaur Gardens Prehistorical Zoo is located ten miles south of Alpena at 11160 US Highway 23 South. There's also an eighteen-hole Raptors Mini-golf. Open seven days a week, from Memorial Day through Labor Day 9:00 a.m. to 6:00 p.m., with shorter hours in May, September, and October. Call (517) 471-5477 or (877) 823-2408, or visit www.dinosaurgardensllc.com. Admission is charged. The repro-duction disclaimer part is more important than you may realize . . . in 1987 one man asked for his money back, disappointed that the dino-saurs weren't real.

"But Officer, This IS the First Time I've . . ."
Roscommon

On May 29, 2002, at approximately 4:20 p.m. in Roscommon County, the unthinkable befell one unsuspecting motorist. After more than thirty years behind the wheel, Bryan Allen Becker of Oakland County was issued his very first one-in-a-million-mile speeding ticket. Not just his first for zipping up Interstate 75 at a 75 mph clip; no, this was his only violation of any kind . . . ever. While this may not seem particularly noteworthy, several reasons validate this story's inclusion.

1. When Becker called the 83rd District Court to learn the fate of his fine at 4:28 p.m. that same day (May 29), a friendly recording answered, informing jurors that all cases for May 9 had been settled. Proceedings would next be scheduled the week of May 16. I guess they believe in giving jurists as much advance notice as possible, although eleven months seems to be stretching it.

2. Further examination revealed that the most prominent speed trap in the state is along Interstate 75 near West Branch. Roscommon runs a close second.

3. State Trooper Keith McCauley, now retired, gained celebrity status in the 1990s for writing more tickets than anyone else. His typical day in Ogemaw County consisted of signing his autograph on twenty-five to thirty numbered, limited edition pieces of paper. According to his buddies, "all of them were good . . . he hardly ever went to court."

4. Unaware that life is moving faster these days, troopers currently hand out on a daily basis something much less, generally around three or four, but that number can go as high as fifteen on weekends when they say, "It's like shooting fish in a barrel."

5. And lastly, the stark reality is that Bryan is my once flawless husband, who now has proved he'll do anything in the pursuit of a good scoop.

index

index

index

index